T0065462

Contents

Little A and Growing Up

An African American Boy and his Grandma

John Chipley

authorHOUSE®

AuthorHouse™
1663 Liberty Drive
Bloomington, IN 47403
www.authorhouse.com
Phone: 833-262-8899

Published by AuthorHouse 06/15/2021

ISBN: 978-1-6655-2889-4 (SC)
ISBN: 978-1-6655-2888-7 (e)

Print information available on the last page.

Any people depicted in stock imagery provided by Getty Images are models, and such images are being used for illustrative purposes only. Certain stock imagery © Getty Images.

This book is printed on acid-free paper.

Because of the dynamic nature of the Internet, any web addresses or links contained in this book may have changed since publication and may no longer be valid. The views expressed in this work are solely those of the author and do not necessarily reflect the views of the publisher, and the publisher hereby disclaims any responsibility for them.

To Henry

A Note from the Author

This is a book for boys trying their best to grow up in a crazy world. A boy's journey into manhood happens regardless of what you or I do or don't do. Along the way he will probably make a lot of mistakes. This is just part of God's plan. Along the way he's going to need help from a lot of people. These people, hopefully, will be good parents, excellent teachers, positive friends, and God. So, to all boys (black, white, or purple), work hard, hang with the right friends, and be what you were created to be. Little A learns a lot about growing up in this book, and so will you.

The Introduction

Papa and Henry have a talk

One day while I was sitting in my garage doing nothing, my grandson, Henry, joined me.

"What ya' do'n Papa?"

"Noth'n, Henry. I'm just sit'n here looking at all the stuff in my shop."

"Papa, are ya' rich? Daddy told me you're rich."

"Well, Henry, compared to some people, I am. Compared to other people, I'm not. What do you think?"

"I think you're rich. You got a big house and lots of cars and stuff."

"Does that make a person rich, Henry?"

"Yep! Sure does. You have lots of money."

"Without you, Henry, I could never be rich. I might have money. But if I didn't have you, I wouldn't be rich. I'd be the poorest person in the world."

"How old are you, Papa?"

"Seventy-eight."

"SEVENTY-EIGHT! Papa, you're old, real old!"

"Papa, would you tell me a story. I love your stories."

"Sure, what kind of story do you want to hear?"

"Tell me a story about you and your Grandma. I love your Grandma stories."

"O.K., young man, pull up a chair. How old are you now, Henry?"

"I'm twelve, Papa. You know that."

"O.K., I'll tell you a story, a TRUE STORY, about Grandma and me when I was your age. Is that O.K.?"

"Sure, but make sure it's true. I really like your true stories. You grew up poor, didn't you?"

"Yes sir! Grandma and I were poor, mighty poor. But I didn't know I was poor. I didn't know what poor was. Now, be quiet and listen to my story. And if you get scared, just tell me to stop, O.K.?"

"O.K., I'll be quiet, Papa. Go ahead, tell me your story."

The Story

Grandma and Me

My name is Abraham. However, Grandma was the only person who ever called me Abraham. Everyone else called me Little A, even my teachers. I was small for my age back then. Today I am large for my age, too large. When I was twelve years old, I lived with my grandma in the inner city of Memphis, in a housing project called Red Oaks. Red Oaks was a place where people lived who couldn't afford to live anywhere else.

Grandma and I lived in a small first-floor apartment. It had two bedrooms, a living room, a small kitchen, and one bathroom. All the rooms were painted the same yucky green color. I called it baby puke green. It was ugly! However, it was home.

One day, when I was at the grocery store with Grandma, I saw a magazine full of houses, big houses. I told Grandma that one day I was going to live in a big house. I'd have a house full of rooms and windows and lots of bathrooms. Plus, I'd have my own basketball goal. I'd play basketball all day, and the big kids won't push me off the court or steal my basketball. Grandma laughed at my dreams, but she worked mighty hard to make sure I kept dreaming.

Grandma was very old. I think she was around eighty years old. She was very proud of her age. Sometimes she told people that she was eighty-five. She was also very smart. She never went to school, not one day. She taught herself how to read, do math, and talk to Jesus. Grandma was a large lady, very large. I think she had only two or three dresses. They all looked the same to me. They were all black with white dots. Her arms were huge and soft. On the outside, she looked old, but she was as smart as a fox on the inside. Grandma always told me that if I could read, do math, and talk to Jesus, I could be anything I wanted to be when I grew up.

Grandma told me I was smart. She didn't tell me that just once, but every day! If someone tells you something every day, over and over, soon you begin to believe it. So, I thought I really was smart. Henry, I hope your mom and dad tell you that you're smart, because you are. I can see it. I've always seen it.

If I ever came home from school with a grade less than an A, Grandma would sit at the kitchen table and just look at me. This hurt me a lot more than any punishment she could have given me. She always said, "Little A, why didn't **WE** make an A? What did **WE** do wrong?" She always said, "**WE**," not "YOU."

My daddy was in prison. He killed a man. He killed his best friend. It's crazy, but it's true. I've never seen my daddy, except in a picture of him hanging on Grandma's bedroom wall. He looked to be around sixteen. Plus, I never knew my mom. She had me when she was just fourteen. As soon as I was born, she tossed me to Grandma and moved to California with her new boyfriend. So, I grew up with my grandma. She turned out to be the best parent a boy could ask for. She was my mom, my friend, and someone I could talk to about anything, **AND I DO MEAN ANYTHING.**

(I paused my story. "Henry, I hope you can talk with your parents about ANYTHING. It's the best gift any parent can give to a child. Grandma gave me this gift when I started school.")

When I started the first grade, Grandma sat me down at the kitchen table and looked straight at me. She was serious! She said, "Little A, you and me, we needs to have a talk." Then she was quiet for a long time. She took a large sip of black coffee to wet her throat, then she told me, "Little A, life is hard and it's not fair. You are black and poor. If you make a mistake, just one, you will wind up in prison. If you make someone mad, they might kill you. Little A, I raised six boys, and your daddy is the only one still alive, and he's in prison."

7

Then she said in a soft whisper, "Little A, I have an idea. **Let's grow up together.** I know I'm an old lady and you be just a young boy, but if you'll let me help you grow up, you can be as smart and as rich as any NBA player. You don't have to live in the projects. You can escape this place. You can have a big house and a fancy car. And I can come live with you and clean your big house.

"Abraham, tomorrow you start the first grade. I can't go with you. I won't be there to help you. When you start school, you gonna meet all kind of boys, good and bad. Soon, child, you be hearing words and seeing things you might not understand. Some of the big boys are going to tell you things that aren't true. Other boys are going to tell you things that will get you in trouble. Abraham, if you are going to college and buy a big house, YOU MUST AVOID TROUBLE. So, here's my plan.

"I want you to ask me anything, about **ANYTHING**. Abraham, I know I'm not a boy. And I know I never went to school, but I'm smart. Abraham, every day when you come home from school, I want us to talk. I want you to tell me about your day and anything that's bothering you, ANYTHING! Will you do that? Will you let me help?"

I wasn't sure I knew what Grandma was talking about. I asked her, "What will we talk about, Grandma?"

Grandma replied, "ANYTHING, Abraham, ANYTHING. When you start school, some of the big boys, the bullies, will say bad things to hurt you. They will try to make you mad. They might say words, bad words, words that you don't understand. I want you to remember those words so we can talk about them when you get home. Some boys use bad words just to show off. This is how you can spot someone you shouldn't hang with. Remember, Abraham, you can ask me any question about anything you don't understand.

Then she told me, "And one more thing, Abraham, NEVER fight, NEVER! When you go to school, sometimes the big boys will say bad things to you. They might even push you around. But you must NEVER fight. If you do, you'll get in trouble. Remember, Abraham, when you walk away from a fight, you win the fight! However, walking away from insults will not be easy, Abraham. It's hard to walk away when people are yelling insults at you, but you have to! If you don't, you will wind up in the principal's office. And that, Abraham, is where the badness starts. The principal will write something about you on your permanent record, something bad. This, Abraham, will hurt my heart."

So, with Grandma's words of wisdom, I started the first grade. I was on my own and excited about being in the first grade. I was only five, but I felt like I was a big boy. I felt like a soldier going off to war. And, in a weird way, that was what happened. I didn't go to my neighborhood school, where all my friends went. I was assigned to a new school outside of our neighborhood. The new school was a long way from where I lived, and I didn't know anyone. I saw mostly white kids, but I also saw a few black kids. However, even the black kids didn't look like me. They looked rich. All the kids at my new school looked rich.

I don't know how to describe what a rich kid looks like. Maybe it was the small things I saw, like clean socks, fancy haircuts, or new shoes that were the right size. As I walked down the hallway on my first day of school, I felt different. I felt like I didn't belong. I also felt like everyone was staring at me, like it was <u>their</u> school, not mine. Their faces were asking me, why was I there?

I'm glad Grandma and I had our talk. She was right about bad kids. On the very first day of school, while I was walking down the hall looking for my classroom, a big white kid bumped into me. I hit the floor hard. My lunch box broke open, and food went everywhere. The big kid looked down at me on the floor and laughed. He told his friends, "Look guys, another little first grade bastard from across town." Then everyone laughed at me. They laughed and walked past me and down the hallway toward the middle school wing. I just sat there on the floor and watched as everyone laughed at me. Then a small white boy with wild red hair stopped and helped me. He said, "Hi, I'm Gilbert, third grade. Welcome to my world. Don't let that big dumb butt bother you. He's dumb as dirt." Then he laughed and said, "See you at lunch. What's your name?"

I replied, "Little A."

Now I had a friend. Thanks to Gilbert, I was feeling a little better about my new school. Then I met my first-grade teacher, Mrs. Bowman. She was wonderful and beautiful and Black. She showed me to my desk and made me feel a lot better. I loved learning. I knew, even at the age of five, that school was my ticket to being whatever I wanted to be in life. With Grandma's help, and constant reminders of how smart I was, how could I possibly NOT be successful. School taught me the three R's, but Grandma taught me about life and people. She taught me two things they don't teach at school: ATTITUDE and CHARACTER. Grandma told me that ATTITUDE is how you see things, and CHARACTER is what you do with what you see.

At first, I didn't understand. However, over time I began to learn the value of both attitude and character.

Grandma always had my back, and I could ask her anything. It made growing up a lot easier.

I think between the first and seventh grade, I heard every bad word there was to hear. I think the kids at my new school used more bad words than the kids in my neighborhood. Grandma and I talked about every word. We even talked about boy stuff words, private words about private parts. Grandma told me to ask her ANYTHING, and that is what I did.

I discovered that when you talk about bad words, and not just say bad words, the bad words aren't so bad. They are just words. Bad words are words usually said in anger. They are words that are usually shouted. They are words that are meant to hurt. This is why they are called BAD WORDS. However, they should be called ANGRY WORDS. The "F word" seemed to be the favorite bad word at my new school. And, yes, Grandma told me all about the "F word."

(I paused my story and looked over at Henry. "Henry, how many bad words do you know?"

"Papa, I'm twelve years old. I know all the bad words, but I don't say them."

"Good. That makes me real proud of you. Now, back to the story.")

Bad Words

When I came home from my first day in the first grade, I already had a question for Grandma. When Grandma asked me how I liked school, I told her I had a question. She stopped what she was doing, and we sat at the kitchen table next to each other. This was something we started doing every day after school. I asked Grandma my first question, "What's a bastard?"

Grandma smiled and said, "First, thank you for asking me. Abraham, the word bastard is usually used as a bad word. However, it is only a word some kids use to make you feel bad. The word bastard is sometimes used to describe a person who was born before their mother was married."

I asked Grandma, "Why is that bad?"

Grandma started to laugh. "Abraham, you are one smart little boy. I do not know why the word bastard is a bad word. Most the kids in our neighborhood are little bastards." Then she laughed. "Abraham, words are not bad. Words are just a way of expressing how someone feels. Words can also tell you a lot about the person using those words. Did someone at school call you a bastard?"

"Yeah."

"Did the students laugh at you?"

"Yeah. It was terrible. Everyone laughed at me. I just sat on the floor and didn't do or say anything."

Grandma smiled. "Good, I'm proud of you. You didn't fight. You didn't say anything bad back to the boy. This means YOU WON! This means you are a better person than he is. Yes, people laughed at you. But the boy who tried to make you feel bad, well, he failed. HE LOST THE GAME."

I asked Grandma why boys used bad words. She said, "Boy, and girls, use bad words because they are hurt'n on the inside. They use words to try to hurt you and make them sound stronger than you. It's sad. So, tomorrow, when you go to school, say something nice about the bad boy to anyone. Kids talk. That bad boy will hear that you said something nice about him. He needs someone to make him feel better about himself."

"What do I say?"

Grandma thought for a few minutes, then said, "I don't know, but you'll think of something. Just be kind."

The next day at school, I saw the same big boy, and he saw me. He started walking in my direction. When he got close to where I was standing, I shouted, "STOP! ARE YOU GOING TO PUSH ME DOWN AGAIN?" The big boy stopped and looked down at me.

I told him that I'd much rather be his friend. His reply was not very friendly, "You little bastard." This time, however, when he said that, another big boy stepped up next to me and told the bad boy to leave me alone. He told the boy that I was just in the first grade. And then he told the boy that he was my friend. The big boy who called me a bastard turned and walked away. He never bothered me again, and I now had another new friend, Ryan. He became like my big brother. Ryan was in the seventh grade. Over time, Ryan and I became good friends. On that day, I never said a bad word back to the big kid. And, as much as I wanted to, I didn't hit the big overgrown bastard. Grandma was right. Grandma was always right. I wondered how she got to be so smart without ever going to school.

School, starting in the first grade, taught me a lot of stuff. I learned grammar, spelling, math, science, and how to get along with other kids. I learned new words – both good and bad. I learned how to use these words to help people. I also admit that I sometimes said some bad words. However, if I did say the wrong word, and it hurt someone, I felt worse than they did. I think that was a good sign. I think it meant I was learning how to use the right words and how to avoid using the bad words.

Grandma taught me that bad words were not a sign that a person was bad. It was a sign that the person was **hurting**.

(I paused my story and looked over at Henry. "Henry, it's hard to spot bad kids. They don't smell bad or look bad. They just do and say bad things. So, be careful who you hang with. REMEMBER, YOU WILL BECOME WHO YOU HANG WITH.

"Henry, this was what Grandma always told me and it's true. Plus, one more thing. Sometimes your best friend can change and become a bad person. Because they are your best friend, you might not see it. So, be careful. Gilbert was my best friend when I was in the first grade, but, over time, he changed. We soon parted ways.)

The Finger

Grandma allowed me to ask the hard questions. There were no rules. All questions were welcomed, even "The Finger" question! I came home from school and sat at the kitchen table. Grandma was, as usual, cooking supper. I sat there, not saying a word. Then I asked Grandma, "Can we talk?"

"Sure, Abraham, what's on your mind." Then she stopped cooking and sat down at the kitchen table. The kitchen table had become our special place where we could talk about anything, ANYTHING!

I asked Grandma, "Why do boys stick their middle finger up in the air at each other? What does it mean?"

"Good question, Abraham. However, I don't have a good answer as to why boys do that. It looks stupid. But I think it's supposed to be like a sign language for the F-word. It's a way of saying a bad word without saying it. I think it is supposed to look like your private parts, but it doesn't. It looks like a finger. However, if a boy is on one side of the classroom and you are on the other side, he can give you the finger. The teacher can't hear anything. However, he just said something. But remember, it's just a finger, nothing more. Do you understand?"

17

Grandma looked over her glasses at me, "So, child, this is just one more stupid little badness thing. I hope you will wave at people and not give them the finger."

Grandma was the smartest person I ever knew, and she never went to school. She educated herself. One day, I asked her how she got to be so smart and never went to school. She told me that the world was her school, and the Lord was her teacher.

Gilbert

Remember Gilbert? He was the boy who helped me on the first day of school. He was in the third grade, and I was in the first grade. Gilbert and I became instant friends. We always sat together at lunch time. At first, Gilbert was like any other third-grade kid. Then he started to change.

One day at lunch, he didn't have any lunch. He told me he lost it while walking to school, so I gave him half of my PB&J. He ate it. He ate it fast, too fast. I asked him if he wanted the other half. He didn't hesitate, "Sure, don't you want it?" Something told me to say, "NO, I'M NOT HUNGRY."

Gilbert grabbed the second half of my sandwich before I could hand it to him. Again, he ate it in just three bites. I then gave him my potato chips and carton of milk. I've never seen a person eat like that. It scared me. When I got home, I told Grandma about Gilbert. The next day, Grandma started fixing extra food for me to take to school for Gilbert. This went on for about a month. Gilbert and I didn't say a word about the food. We just enjoyed it. This is what friends do. Then I noticed something else.

One day at lunch, I saw small black bugs crawling around in Gilberts wild red hair. Gilbert NEVER combed his hair. It stood out and went in all directions. When I saw the bugs, I realized he never washed his hair. In fact, I could tell he never washed – PERIOD! When I got home, I told Grandma. She said that maybe he was homeless. He might be sleeping in a car or something like that. Grandma called the school and talked to the guidance counselor. The counselor told Grandma that she didn't have time to check up on where all the students slept. She also told Grandma it wasn't any of her business. I watched as Grandma started to cry. She told me that Gilbert needed our help, but she didn't know how to help him.

The next day at lunch, I noticed Gilbert had red marks on his arms. When I asked him about the marks, he just looked at me and said, "I'm sorry." Then he stood up and walked out of the lunchroom. Then, I watched as he walked down the hallway and out of the school.

I asked my teacher why Gilbert went home. She took me into the teacher's lounge and over to a quiet area where we could talk. She told me that Gilbert had problems at home. She told me that was all she was allowed to say. Then she told me that he was being transferred to another school. I found out from some of the older kids at school that Gilbert had been transferred to Westmore Elementary / Middle School.

Westmore was more like a prison than a school. If a kid had problems when they were transferred to Westmore, they would have a lot more problems when they got out. Gilbert was small, but he had a temper. About two weeks ago, I heard from a kid in the neighborhood, who also went to Westmore, that Gilbert peed on his teacher and was expelled.

Seven years ago, in the first grade, was the last time I saw Gilbert, until today! While walking home from school, I took a shortcut down Tillman Street. I knew not to go down Tillman Street. It wasn't a safe place to be, but I was in a hurry and decided to go where I shouldn't have gone. That was when I saw Gilbert.

He was a long way away, but it was Gilbert. He was sitting on the top of a tall brick wall, a wall full of graffiti. The graffiti wall was how the gangs communicated with each other. Gilbert, with his wild red hair, was easy to spot sitting on the wall. As I got closer, I could see Gilbert more clearly. He was covered in street dirt. His red hair was matted, and his clothes were dirty. I could actually smell him as well as see him. Then Gilbert saw me.

I called out his name, "**GILBERT?**"

He jumped down off the wall and swaggered over to where I was standing. "MY NAME AIN'T GILBERT, BOY, IT'S PIT BULL!"

I quickly replied, "Chill, it's me, Little A."

"I KNOW WHO YOU ARE! WHY ARE YOU ON TILLMAN? YOU KNOW THIS AIN'T YOUR STREET."

I ignored his warning, and asked, "Gilbert, I mean PIT BULL, how are you doing?"

He didn't reply. He just stood there staring at me. I suddenly realized what a stupid question that was. Then he quickly replied, "WHAT DO YOU THINK, SHIT-ASS?" I didn't have to ask him if he were hungry, I could see that with my eyes. PIT BULL looked just like his new name. He looked bad and angry. Or maybe he was bad because he was angry. And, maybe he was angry because he was hungry.

I asked him if he wanted to come home with me for a snack. His expression changed. His eyes became sharp. Suddenly, I became afraid.

PIT BULL took a step closer to me, too close. "LITTLE A, IF I WANTED YOUR DAMN FOOD, I'D JUST TAKE IT. DO YOU UNDERSTAND, BOY? I DON'T NEED YOUR CHARITY! I MAKE MORE MONEY IN A WEEK THAN YOU DO IN A YEAR!"

Then he turned around and climbed back up on top of the wall. When he did that, I saw a pistol butt pushing out from under his sweatshirt. When I saw that, I knew I was in the wrong place at the wrong time. I also knew that PIT BULL could explode on me at any minute. His rotten teeth told me he was on something bad, probably meth. I had to leave, and I had to leave NOW!

I said, "I understand, PIT BULL." then I slowly started backing away. I tried to look like I was not backing away. However, my eyes could not stop staring at PIT BULL and his pistol, a Glock. I wanted to help him, but I was also afraid to help. Gilbert looked like a timebomb ready to go off. He looked angry, and he had a reason to look angry. No one helped him when he needed help. Schools expelled him. Foster families abused him. His only family was now the gang that controlled Tillman Street.

I inched my way backward, turned around, and slowly started walking away. I could feel his eyes watching my every step. I was scared, very scared. I could hardly keep my legs from falling out from under me. As I walked away, I listened carefully for the sound of a click coming from his gun. There was nothing I could do but walk and listen. If I heard a clicking sound, I knew Gilbert was getting ready to kill me. All I could do was walk and pray. And that is what I did all the way home. Every time I walked under a pair of tennis shoes hanging from an overhead line, I prayed a little louder and walked a little faster.

When I got home, Grandma was waiting for me. I was late coming home from school, and she was worried. When Grandma saw me coming down the street, she went inside to start supper.

The Badness

When I got home, I sat down at the kitchen table as I always did. It was my one-on-one time with Grandma. We did this every day when I got home from school. However, today was a little different. Grandma asked, "Abraham, why ya so late get'n home from school? I was get'n a little worried."

I didn't answer Grandma at first. Then Grandma stopped cooking, wiped her hands off on a dish rag, and sat in the chair next to mine. She leaned over close to me and whispered, "What's wrong Abraham?"

Again, I didn't reply at first, but Grandma waited for my reply. She must have waited thirty minutes. She didn't say a word, not one word. Then I slowly started talking. "Grandma, do you remember the funny looking little boy I ate lunch with back in the first grade, the boy with the wild red hair, Gilbert?"

Grandma laughed, "Gilbert! The white boy, skinny as a rail. You done gave him food at lunch every day. The poor little thing was starved. He was a strange boy. I think you told me he was transferred to Westmore. That was a long time ago, Abraham."

I looked over at Grandma, "Well, Grandma, he's back."

Grandma looked shocked, "Is he back at your school?"

"No," I hesitated. Then said, "No, he's back on Tillman Street."

Grandma continued to wipe her hands on a towel, "Tillman? Then he's in a gang, right?"

"Yeah. He has a new street name, **PIT BULL**. I saw him today. That's why I was late coming home from school. Grandma, he's not Gilbert anymore."

Grandma took a deep breath and let it out slowly, "Abraham, child, we don't talk as much as we used to talk. When you were a little boy, you shared everything with me. When you turned ten years old, you started telling me less and less. I could tell you was not saying everything. I understand. You're growing up so fast. You're learning how to make decisions on your own. All this is good.

"But, Abraham, I also know 'The Feeling.' I know the feeling that a grandma gets when things aren't right. I know the feeling when words are **not** said. Abraham, I know that feeling, and I'm get'n that feeling. So, child, tell me why I'm get'n that feeling."

When Grandma said that, tears slowly started running down my face. Then, I began to cry and couldn't stop. Grandma let me cry. Somehow, she knew I was struggling with something. She also knew if I wanted to tell her something, I'd tell her. She knew that growing up wasn't easy. Grandma knew I was just like a little bird trying to jump out of the nest and fly. So, she just reached over with her large soft arms and held me. She didn't say a word. She waited for me to tell her what I was crying about.

I couldn't look at Grandma. I just looked at the floor. "It's not Gilbert's fault. I'm mad, Grandma, I'm mad! People turned Gilbert into PIT BULL. He never had a chance. Grandma, I've got to try to help Gilbert. If I don't try to help him, that makes me as bad as everyone else. Grandma, I've got to try."

Grandma let go of me and sat up straight. She made me look at her. "Abraham, look at me. Gilbert isn't Gilbert anymore, and it's not your fault. Gilbert is PIT BULL. He belongs to a gang. Abraham, you can't change some things. If you try to change PIT BULL, he might strike at you or kill you. There are some bad things in life we have to accept. This, child, is one of those things. Abraham, don't try to make Gilbert what you want him to be. Let him make his own decisions. Okay?"

I listened to Grandma, but what Grandma didn't know was the look I saw on PIT BULL's face. I had to do something. I had to try to save Gilbert. I cried because I had never seen what "the badness" looked like on the face of a young boy. It scared me. I knew if I didn't do something to help Gilbert, something Grandma called 'the badness' was going to explode inside his gut. And, when that happens, a lot of people would get hurt.

(I stopped telling my story and looked over at Henry. I told Henry when I was his age, I lived in a crazy world. I saw too many Pit Bulls walking the streets. I saw their glassy eyes and their angry faces. I saw the swagger in their walk. I heard it in their hateful words. I saw evil tattoos on their bodies. So, where did all this badness come from? When I asked adults why some boys were so bad, they would say things like, "The boy was just born bad."

I didn't like that answer. So, I would tell the adults, "__NO, WRONG__! No boy is born bad. Badness is learned. It comes from people, people like you. God don't make no junk, __YOU DO__." Henry was as quiet as a church mouse. He was glued to every word. He motioned for me to continue. So, I continued my story.)

Pit Bull

Like all boys, I began to change with age. I slowly started keeping more and more things to myself. Grandma was getting older. She started using a walking cane, and she started telling me the same stories over and over. I was now beginning to look after Grandma more than she was looking after me. We were both getting older, and we were both changing.

I was now learning how to be independent. I was learning how to make my own decisions. I was learning how to choose my friends. I was learning how to discover who I was and what I wanted to be when I grew up. And I mastered the art of survival on the streets of Binghampton.

As much as I loved Grandma, I told her less and less. I was a boy learning how to be a man. I was now twelve years old. There were things I had to do on my own. And the number one thing I did every day was get along with some very tough kids at school and in my neighborhood. In the hood, all the boys played a part, like in the movies. One of these boys was PIT BULL. However, as I've already said, PIT BULL was just his street name. His real name was Gilbert. And, like far too many boys, Gilbert learned how to raise himself. He now belonged to a gang of boys who lived on Tillman Street. Or maybe I should say, they owned Tillman Street. No one went down Tillman Street without their approval.

After my run-in with PIT BULL, I knew I had to do something to help him. Grandma told me to allow Gilbert to be PIT BULL. She was afraid that PIT BULL was going to hurt me or, maybe, kill me. She also told me that I did not have the right to make people what I wanted them to be. I listened to Grandma, but I also listened to my heart. I knew what I had to do. I had to try to save Gilbert.

That night, at the dinner table, it was a cold and quiet supper. Grandma didn't feel like cooking, and I didn't feel like eating. When supper was over, I didn't work on my homework. I wasn't able to think about school stuff. All I could think about was Gilbert. So, I went to my room where I could be alone and think. In a few minutes, I returned to the kitchen. Grandma was still washing dishes. She always worked. She didn't move as fast as she used to, but she never stopped working. I sat at the kitchen table and waited for her to finish. She knew I was there, but she pretended to not see me. She just hummed hymns and washed dishes.

Grandma didn't look at me. She didn't say a word. When Grandma finally put away the last dish, she walked over and sat at the table in the chair next to me. She still didn't say a word. She just sat there and waited for me to say what I needed to say. She just silently waited until I was ready to say it.

I finally told Grandma what happened. I told her everything. I told her that I asked Gilbert to come home with me and get a snack. I told Grandma that Gilbert yelled, **"If I wanted your damn food, I'd just take it!"**

Grandma looked over at me, held up her hand, and said, "Stop!" Then she sat silently for a long time not saying a word. I didn't know what she was going to say, so I said nothing. I just sat there. Finally, Grandma said in a very quiet voice, a voice that was slow in coming, one word at a time, "Abraham, if we do noth'n, someone is going to get hurt. If we do something, Pit Bull will hurt you.

"Do you see my problem? You want to help, but Gilbert don't want your help. Gilbert has the badness deep down inside his soul. Once a boy gets the badness that deep down inside his soul, it's hard to get it out; it be real hard. It's like a cancer. Little A, when a boy catches the badness, it will grow and grow and grow until it kills all the goodness.

"Child, listen to me and listen good. Gilbert don't want to be Gilbert anymore. Gilbert wants to be PIT BULL. He may look your age, but he already be a man. He be a fourteen-year-old man. And that, Abraham, is both sad and dangerous. Life has poisoned him. Life has filled him with the badness. That be all he can see."

Again, Grandma stopped talking. This time, she folded her hands together and started to pray. I couldn't hear what she and God were talking about, but Grandma's voice kept getting louder and louder. Then, it suddenly stopped. While her head was still bowed in prayer, she pointed to the closet and her purse, the bright red purse, the one with a wooden cross on the side.

"Abraham," she said in a voice so slow every word was a sentence, "fetch - me – my- healing - purse." When I returned with her healing purse, Grandma told me to follow her and show her where I saw Gilbert. She told me if we find Gilbert to not say a word, NOT ONE WORD! Then she grabbed my face with both hands, stared at me. She said, "Abraham, if we find Gilbert, and I tell you to leave, **you leave.** Ya' hear me? You leave! And, if I tell you to run, **ya' run!** These are my rules. Do you understand?"

All I could say was, "Yes' m." And with those instructions, Grandma and I marched out the front door of our apartment. I was scared. I could feel that something bad was about to happen. I just didn't know what that "something" was.

It was starting to get dark. It was that time of day when most people were going inside and locking their doors. It was also that time of day when gangs, like nocturnal animals, came out of their hiding places and defended their turf. Then, suddenly, it started to rain. She walked slowly with her cane and her large red healing purse. I followed behind, not knowing what was about to happen. The sun was almost gone, and the rain was getting stronger. Grandma didn't seem to notice either. She just kept walking, and I kept following her steps.

As Grandma and I approached the wall, Pit Bull was gone. So, we walked down Tillman Street looking for Gilbert. However, the streets were his home. He knew every inch. He was good at not being found. We looked for over an hour. The rain was now coming down harder. Then, about two blocks ahead of us, I saw him. PIT BULL was standing with some bigger boys at a corner store. I pointed him out to Grandma. She took one look and told me to leave. She told me that I would embarrass him in front of his gang. This would cause the badness to leap out.

I didn't want to leave Grandma, but she reminded me of our agreement. I didn't want to leave, but Grandma was tough. She was also a lot smarter than the gang boys. She was like a rattlesnake. She would wait for the right time to strike. Timing was everything.

I also knew that Grandma might get hurt if I didn't leave. So, just as I promised, I went home and waited. I waited for a long time, too long. However, I didn't know what I was waiting for. I didn't know what Grandma was going to do. And I was afraid to think of what PIT BULL and his gang might do to Grandma. All I could do was wait, and that is what I did. I waited. I sat in the dark at the kitchen table and waited. It was the worse night of my life. It was also the longest night. My fear grew with the sound of every police car. I can remember watching the clock on the kitchen wall. I watched as the second hand clicked slowly. It was now dark, and the rain was coming down even harder. Something was wrong!

I continued to sit in the dark. I didn't turn on a light or watch TV. I didn't eat. My life stopped. Grandma had been gone a long time, too long. No one should be out on the streets of Binghampton after the sun goes down, no one! I had just decided to call the police when the front door opened. There stood Grandma, soaking wet. Behind Grandma stood Gilbert. He looked like a very wet, shaggy, red- headed dog.

I jumped up and turned on some lights. He didn't say a word, but his body language was full of expression. Just like at school, he didn't talk. He just pointed for what he wanted. I didn't know who I was looking at, PIT BULL or Gilbert. Whoever that person was, standing next to Grandma, he walked into the kitchen and sat across the table from me. HE DIDN'T SAY ONE WORD! Grandma asked me to make some sandwiches while she changed out of her wet clothes. After Grandma left the room, Gilbert said in a cold voice, "I have a gun."

I replied, "I know. I saw it." The room remained silent while I started making sandwiches. Then I heard Gilbert say, "I need to hide it."

I tried to look cool and replied, "Large cookie jar, top shelf."

Gilbert stood up, removed the pistol from under his shirt, and placed it in the cookie jar. Then he returned to the kitchen table and sat down. He refused to make eye contact with me. I didn't know what to say. Then Gilbert finally started talking.

"Little A, when I saw you on Tillman Street, I didn't recognize you at first. But I saw your Jordans. I was going to kill you. I saw you coming long before you saw me. I was going to kill you just for your shoes, and then I recognized you. Then you invited me home for a snack.

Do you remember when you were in the first grade and I was in the third? Do you remember how I always ate your lunch? You never said a word, NEVER! Little A, that was the only food I ever got most days. You didn't know that. You were just a kid, a little boy. Little A, you cared more about me back then than all the adults who moved me from school to school and foster home to foster home. After they moved me to Westmore, I never saw you again until you came down Tillman Street. I was going to kill you. Then I remembered you. I remembered the food you gave me, and how you never made me feel like you were giving me food.

"Little A, I'm not the same little boy anymore. I'm not Gilbert anymore. I'm PIT BULL. I know how to kill people, and I can kill you. I can kill your Grandma. I'm not Gilbert anymore. Do not trust me. I am crazy. Do you understand what I am saying? I AM NOT WHO YOU THINK I AM."

I decided to see if PIT BULL could once again be Gilbert. So, I said, "PIT BULL, I know you're crazy. I know you peed on one of your teachers. You'd have to be crazy to do that." Then I started to laugh. It was a test to see what he would do or say. That was when I wondered if I had gone too far. Then, like a prayer being answered, I heard Gilbert start to laugh. I had never heard Gilbert laugh before. But he laughed then, and then we laughed together. While we laughed, PIT BULL's attitude changed. Grandma walked into the kitchen and asked what was so funny. I told her, "Peeing on your teacher is funny." Grandma said, "I'll pretend I didn't hear that." This made Gilbert and me laugh even harder.

Grandma and her healing purse had changed PIT BULL. I never learned what she did. She never told me what she did. Gilbert couldn't explain what she did. But PIT BULL was changing back into Gilbert. After he had eaten several sandwiches, Grandma told us to take a shower and go to bed. Gilbert looked both dirty and exhausted. He took his shower first. Grandma was also tired. She just put the dishes in the sink and went to bed. This is something she never did. When she did that, I knew something was wrong.

So, I got up and washed the dishes. As I washed the dishes, I kept thinking about Gilbert and/or PIT BULL. Then I looked over and saw the cookie jar. It had been moved. It was now on the middle shelf. I stood up and walked over to the jar. I opened the top of the cookie jar and looked inside. The gun was gone. Then I heard PIT BULLS's voice from behind me, "Little A, don't turn around. I told you I'm not who you think I am."

I didn't turn around. I stood facing the kitchen wall and the empty cookie jar. That was when I heard a clicking sound. I didn't have to look. I knew it was the sound of a Glock getting ready to be fired. I froze and held onto the kitchen counter. I waited. Then I heard PIT BULL's voice, "Sorry, Little A. I can't do it. I just can't do it. I'm sorry. Little A, don't come down Tillman Street anymore. It's not safe, you know that. They'll kill you."

Then PIT BULL said, "I took a pair of your tennis shoes."

Then I heard PIT BULL un-cock his pistol. He didn't say another word. He just turned and walked out of the kitchen. Then I heard the door shut. I never saw him again, but I did see my shoes (or his shoes). PIT BULL took my favorite pair of shoes, Jordans Dub Zero shoes. They were a Christmas gift from Grandma. It took her all year long to save up enough money to buy me that pair of Jordans.

About two weeks later, I was walking home from school with my friend Artez. He stopped walking and pointed up. Above us, hanging from a wire, I saw my shoes. Artez said, "Look, they're Jordans, just like yours. Some poor sucker was killed for a pair of damn tennis shoes."

I never told anyone about PIT BULL taking my shoes. Grandma and I were the only people who knew about PIT BULL taking my shoes. When a gang member is killed, his shoes are tied together and tossed over a street wire. It was a sign to other gangs. I think PIT BULL put on my new Air Jordans, and someone else wanted them. I think my new shoes cost Gilbert his life.

When I got home from school, I saw a box of shoes sitting on the front porch. I opened the box and saw a pair of old dirty tennis shoes. A note was inside the box. It read, "Little A, tell your Grandma it worked. I changed. I changed while walking home from your apartment. I had to leave Tillman Street. It cost me your Air Jordans, but I'm O.K. They didn't kill me. Tell your grandma thanks. And thanks for the PB&J when we were in the first and third grade."

Grandma and her healing purse worked miracles. I don't know how, but somehow it worked. Beneath all the dirt and all the badness, there was still a boy named Gilbert. On that dark rainy night, Grandma did her magic. However, it wasn't magic. It was Grandma.

I took the old tennis shoes inside and showed Grandma the note from Gilbert. She stopped cooking supper and sat down at the kitchen table next to me. Tears filled her eyes. "I was lucky, Abraham, very lucky. However, I think your PB&J sandwiches, back when you were in the first grade, were what really changed Gilbert, not me. Kindness from one boy to another is powerful goodness.

You should feel proud of what you did. I know I'm proud of you."

Then Grandma reached over and gave me one of her giant hugs. There is nothing better than one of Grandma's hugs, not even a new pair of Air Jordans.

Then she said, "So, child, as you start grow'n up, remember Gilbert and PIT BULL. And remember your own special magic of kindness."

(That was the end of my first story. The shop became very quiet. Henry was sitting next to me. He was silent for a long time. Then he said, "I liked that story, Papa, but it was sad. Was it really true?"

I answered, "Yes Sir, Henry, it was true." Then I asked Henry if he knew any boys like Gilbert. He said, "Yeah. I know a lot of Gilbert's at my school, and they all act just like PIT BULL. Now I think I know why. Thanks Papa.")

Another time,
Another story

(One Saturday, Henry and I were working in the yard. I paid him to help me do some of the things I couldn't do anymore. I was beginning to be an old man. It was a win-win deal. I needed help in the yard, and he needed money. This next story started while we watched a boy jogging past my house where we were working. He looked like a good kid. He always waved and said hello to me, and I always returned the kindness. Henry asked me who the boy was. I told him I didn't know his name, but he reminded me of a friend I had growing up. Henry stopped working and sat down on the ground. "Okay, Papa, it's time for another story. Tell me about your friend.")

Dee, Me, Gangs and Roscoe

In the eighth grade, I met a boy named DeQuavious, street name Dee. He was a good kid and very funny. He always wore crazy looking clothes. Plus, he was a great basketball player. He didn't look like a good basketball player, but he was. If he had the ball, he could hit the basket from almost anywhere on the court. However, his grades were not so good. Or, maybe I should say, his grades were terrible, all F's and D's. My grades, on the other hand, were all A's.

DeQuavious called me a nerd, and I called him dumb butt. We both laughed and continued insulting each other daily. We became very good friends one insult at a time. I insulted only my friends. It was like a contest as to who could come up with the best insult or the most gross one.

One Saturday, while shooting baskets, Dee told me that the principal was going to send him to an alternative school because of his grades. He had only one semester to improve his grades, or he was gone.

When Dee said that, I told him I could make him an A student, but he had to help me with my shooting game. He agreed, and we went to work. The first thing I did was to tell Dee that he was already an A student, he just didn't know it. Of course, Dee didn't believe me. So, I asked Dee to give me one week as his tutor, and he agreed. We started immediately. We started with our weekend homework assignment. Our teacher asked us to write a one-page paper on someone we admired. Dee wrote his paper about his mother. I read what he wrote and handed it back to him. Then I asked him to rewrite it. **HE WAS SHOCKED**. He asked, "Why?"

I told him that the first time you write a paper, you will earn a D. Your paper will be too short, look sloppy, and have too many misspelled words. It tells the teacher that you did as little as you could do.

The second time you write it, you check your spelling and make your letters neater. This time you will earn a C. Your paper will now look like all the other papers. It will be neater and have fewer misspelled words.

The third time you rewrite it, it will earn a B or A. The teacher will see that you did more than she asked you to do. Every time you rewrite a paper, your grade will go up. Needless to say, Dee did **not** like my instructions, but he did it. That was our agreement. When we got our papers back, he earned a grade of A. He couldn't believe it! His teacher couldn't believe it. In fact, she thought someone else had written his paper for him. So, we invited our teacher to join us after school so she could see and understand what Dee was doing. Starting the next day, Dee and I did our homework every day in class after school. The teacher watched us while she worked in her classroom. She was impressed!

Dee now understood that he was smart. He just had to learn how to show the teacher how smart he was. He learned a simple lesson. He learned that spending more time on his schoolwork improved his grades. Dee was excited! He was off and running. In fact, he was so excited about being an A student, he almost stopped playing basketball after school. Dee learned that being smart was not a trick. People are **not** born smart or dumb. It all depends on where you spend your time. Once he saw how easy it was to make A's, he was hooked. Dee and I now competed both academically and on the basketball court. And I wish that was the end of this story, but it's not.

Dee and I played basketball with a boy named Tee. That was his street name because he was very tall. He was older than Dee and me, and he was a great basketball player. He was also a nice kid. We were all very tight.

We played basketball every Saturday at the local park. However, Tee's older brother belonged to a street gang. They didn't mess with us because Tee was a younger brother. The gangs ruled the neighborhood. They were well organized and provided both protection and income for their members. I never joined a gang. I just stayed out of their way. Tee, Dee, and I didn't need to join a gang. We had Grandma. If Grandma was on your side, you were O.K. Grandma had her healing purse, and inside her healing purse she had Roscoe. (I don't think I need to tell you what Roscoe was). No one messed with Grandma. She looked like a sweet old lady, but that sweet old lady was big. And she could hurt you if she wanted to.

One Saturday afternoon, after shooting baskets, we all went over to Mr. Lang's store. He usually gave us free Cokes and a snack bar. On that Saturday, Tee slipped a candy bar off the shelf and into his pocket. Then he walked out of the store. Mr. Lang saw him do it but didn't say anything. I walked over to the counter and handed Mr. Lang a dollar. Mr. Lang told me to keep my money, but he told me to be careful. He told me that Tee had probably joined a gang. Stealing a candy bar was usually their first test. Mr. Lang told me, "Little A, if they went fishing for Tee, you and Dee will be their next rats. Please don't do it. These are bad boys. Don't become one of them."

I looked at Mr. Lang. He had a strange look on his face. He looked scared, and he also looked sad. Then he quietly said, "Please, Little A, don't do it. Someone is going to get hurt, and I don't want it to be you."

Tee and Dee left Mr. Lang's store and started walking toward our apartments. Dee yelled out for me to join them. I ran to catch up, but I didn't know what to say. Everything happened so fast. I finally said what I had to say, "Tee, why did you steal the candy bar?" Tee stopped walking. He stared down at me and said, "Are you stupid? You know why I took it. Do you have a problem with it?"

I replied, "No." Then I said, "Yes, I do have a problem with it. If you are joining a gang, I'm going to have to stop shooting baskets with you, and I'm going to hate that. However, I can't afford to get arrested. One day, I'm going to college. If I get arrested, I won't be allowed into any college. Tee, you are still my friend, O.K.? But I am going to college."

Tee replied, "No. I can't be your friend. We're different." Then he turned and walked away. In about two weeks, I saw Dee taking a candy bar. I asked him, "Why?" I told him he was now an A student. I told him that he could go to college.

Dee said, "Little A, you're stupid. You won't go to college, and I won't go to college. We're Black and poor.

Do you understand. Little A, we are who we are. If I don't join a gang, they will make my life Hell. I'm not concerned about college. College is for the rich white kids. I'm concerned about today. Little A, you should also be concerned about today."

I just stood there. My best friend had changed. He looked the same on the outside, but he was not the same on the inside. I told Dee, "NO! I can't. Joining a gang will get me into trouble and keep me from getting into college. However, we can still be friends, O.K.?"

Soon after our talk, Dee stopped doing his homework with me after school, and his grades started to drop. One day at school, while passing in the hallway, Dee slipped me a note. It read, "Tell Mr. Lang to be careful tonight." When I got home from school, Grandma and I had another talk, a serious talk.

I know it's hard for most boys to believe that I can talk to my Grandma about anything, but it's true. We made that agreement when I started the first grade. It was like a gift from her to me, and it was a wonderful gift. When I got home from school, I went into the kitchen and sat down at the table. I told Grandma, "Grandma, we need to talk."

She immediately stopped cooking, dried her hands on a towel, and sat next to me at the table. She asked, "What, child?"

I couldn't look at her. I just looked at the floor and replied, "Dee gave me a note today in school. He told me to tell Mr. Lang to be careful tonight. You know what that means."

Grandma sat quietly for a long time without saying a word. Then she said, "Abraham, our talks keep getting more and more serious, don't they? I thought you were going to ask me something about your private parts, or something really important." Then she laughed, and I laughed. Then we both stopped laughing and just looked at each other. Grandma said, "Okay, Abraham, I think tonight I need to take my healing purse and help Mr. Lang with his inventory."

I quickly replied, "**NO, Grandma!** That's not a good idea. Gangs aren't afraid of you. You'll get hurt."

Grandma smiled and said, "Abraham, just trust in the Lord. I trust in the Lord and my healing purse. I'll be fine." Then she laughed, stood up, and finished cooking supper. I worked on my homework as she continued cooking. She started humming church songs. I didn't know what to feel. I just followed Grandma's advice and trusted in the Lord.

After supper, she asked me to do the dishes for her, finish my homework, and go to bed at my normal bedtime. Then she asked me to fetch her the healing purse. She told me that she might be gone all night. Then she put on her Sunday hat, the one she always wore to church, picked up her healing purse, and walked out the front door. She was calm and still humming church songs.

For the first time, I disobeyed Grandma. I didn't do the dishes, and I didn't do my homework. I waited for Grandma to get out of sight. Then I grabbed my baseball bat from the floor of my closet and ran out the front door. I wasn't going to miss this for anything! And, if Grandma needed help, I would be there for her. I ran around the back side of the block to avoid Grandma and hid next to the store in a dark area behind the ice machine. I could see everything from where I was hiding, but I thought she couldn't see me. I no sooner sat down before I saw her coming. She was slowly walking down the street toward Mr. Lang's store. She was using her cane and not in a hurry. She was still singing hymns.

Grandma arrived at Mr. Lang's store around six o'clock. I could hear everything from where I was hiding. Grandma told Mr. Lang that he might have a problem tonight, and she would like to prevent a problem before someone got hurt. Then she pulled up a chair where she could be seen by anyone entering the store. She made herself comfortable and laid her healing purse in her lap where it was easy to see. The gang arrived early. They entered the store around seven o'clock.

One boy guarded the door, while the rest marched into the store like an army. Dee was one of the solders. Then they saw Grandma. They also saw the healing purse. One of the boys in the gang looked over at Grandma, laughed, and said, "Old lady, what the Hell are you going to do, hit us with your purse?"

Grandma smiled, slowly reached into her healing purse, and pulled out Roscoe.

Grandma said, "Well, it all depends on what you do."

The boy stopped laughing and said, "I've heard about you. You're Little A's crazy grandma. You're crazy as a goat, aren't you?"

Grandma continued to smile, "Boy, you might say that."

Then the boy told the other boys to take whatever they wanted, it's free. That was when Grandma picked up Roscoe and pointed it at the gang leader. Then she slowly pulled back on the hammer. It made a loud clicking noise. Roscoe was a huge pistol with a very long barrel, very long. When Grandma picked up Roscoe, the store got quiet, very quiet. When Grandma pulled back on the hammer, everyone heard the loud clicking sound, a very loud clicking sound. Grandma didn't say a word. The boys froze. The gang leader reached over and took a beer out of the cooler. When he did that, Grandma told him to not move. Then she told him to hold the beer still so she could get a good shot. The boy laughed, but he looked scared. He held the beer away from his body. He jokingly asked, "Is this good enough old lady?"

That was when Grandma pulled the trigger. Roscoe sounded like a bomb going off. Grandma missed the target by a mile, but she got the attention of everyone. Grandma shouted, "HOLD STILL, BOY!" Then she pulled back on the hammer again and took aim. She yelled again, "HOLD STILL, NOW!" When she said that, all the boys started backing out of the store one-by-one. Soon there was only one boy left, the big one, the gang leader, the one holding the beer. He stood there staring at Grandma. Then Grandma pointed Roscoe directly at him and asked, "How big is your gun?"

The big boy yelled, "OLD LADY, I'LL GET YOU FOR THIS!"

Grandma replied, "I know. But today is my day! Now, take off your pants."

"WHAT?" The boy shouted. "NO WAY OLD LADY!"

That was when Grandma pulled the trigger a second time. The bullet hit the beer bottle dead center. The big boy quickly dropped to the floor and pulled off his pants. Then he stood up, wearing only his boxers. "OLD LADY, I SWEAR, I'M GOING TO GET YOU FOR THIS, YOU OLD BITCH!"

Then he turned and ran out of the store. Grandma asked Mr. Lang to pick the boy's pants up off the floor and take out his wallet. Then she called the police and gave them all the information they needed, along with his pants. He was easy to spot by the cops. Not many boys walk down the street in just their boxers.

He and all the gang members were arrested and went before a judge. However, Mr. Lang refused to press charges. Instead, he told the boys, if they were ever hungry, to come to his store and he would give them food. And maybe, if they had time, they could help him put up stock.

Mr. Lang was a very wise old man. Instead of prosecuting the boys, he developed a friendship with them. They never took things from his store again. In fact, they protected his store from other gangs. Dee was one of the boys who got arrested. After what Mr. Lang did, Dee started staying after school. We, once again, started working on our homework together. Yes, his grades improved. Yes, this story does have a happy ending. And, yes, Grandma got home okay that night. I ran to beat her home and jumped in bed. When she got home, she came into my bedroom and poked me with her cane. She laughed and told me to sit up. She knew I was pretending to be asleep. She told me she knew I was there. From where she was sitting, she could see me hiding behind the ice machine. She also told me, "Abraham, we have to talk." I asked her if everything was okay. All she told me was, "Tomorrow, Abraham, we have to talk tomorrow."

We Have to Talk

That next morning Grandma said, "Abraham, it's called fishing."

"What do you mean fishing, Grandma?"

Grandma sat across the kitchen table from me. Over the years, Grandma and I had many kitchen table talks. Some were just talks, others were more serious. On that morning, Grandma looked serious as we started our talk.

"Abraham, you do know we have a problem, right?"

I replied, "No! What kind of problem, Grandma?"

"It's Dee. I was looking out the window yesterday and watched as he delivered a dime-pack of drugs to another boy, a boy much younger. Abraham, Dee is running drugs. I think you know this, and he is still part of a gang. Abraham, they are going to come after you. I remember when they came after my boys. My boys promised me they would never join a gang, but they did. I didn't know it until they were arrested. Abraham, do you belong to a gang? Please, tell me the truth."

"NO, Grandma! I don't belong to a gang. I've got you and Roscoe. I don't need a gang." Then I started to laugh, but Grandma didn't laugh.

"Abraham, it's not funny. You are like a fish in a pond, and they are going to keep fishing until they catch you. And, if they don't catch you, they will make your life pure Hell. Once they start, they don't stop until they catch their fish. Twelve-year-old boys, like you, are perfect fish, and just waiting to be caught.

"Abraham, Dee is still in a gang. I know you and Dee are friends. However, Dee will be getting a lot of pressure to go fishing for you. He will get some kind of reward for getting you to join. Abraham, I also know it's normal for boys your age to start making their own decisions. What I'm saying, Abraham, is if you do join a gang, I probably won't know it.

"Abraham, we've been talking at this kitchen table every day after school for almost seven years. Now it's time for us to really trust each other. I know Dee is running drugs. And I know that you and Dee are good friends and spend a lot of time together. But remember this, if you are standing with him when he hands a dime-pack to another boy and gets caught, you will go to jail with him. Do you understand how serious this is? You will be found guilty due to association.

"Abraham, you're an A student. One day you will be going to college. Dee's bad decision to join a gang might take you down with him. It will happen fast. Your life will change instantly. What do you think we should do?"

"Grandma, Dee is my friend. We do homework together, shoot baskets together, but I will never join a gang, Grandma, NEVER."

Grandma replied, "Abraham, you didn't hear me. You don't have to join a gang. You only need to be with him when he has drugs on him. What if you are shooting baskets and Dee has a pack on him to deliver later that day? The cops know Dee belongs to a gang. They are not stupid. They know every boy in this neighborhood. They probably watch Dee and all the other gang members every day. Abraham, a boy in the projects, if arrested, doesn't have a chance. It's not fair but it is what it is. If you go to jail, it's a one way trip."

"What are you saying, Grandma?"

"I'm saying, I think we need to move, or you need to move. Too many boys in this neighborhood belong to gangs. Sooner or later something bad is going to happen. I can feel it in my bones. If the police don't get you, a gang member will. If we stay where we are, and you hang with the boys in this neighborhood, sooner or later you will get arrested for just being in the wrong place at the wrong time. Do you understand?"

"NO! I DON'T UNDERSTAND. I LIKE MY FRIENDS AT SCHOOL. I DON'T WANT TO MOVE. I WON'T GO! GRANDMA, I WON'T GO!"

Grandma stood up from the kitchen table. She looked down at me, then she got mad and in my face. "Abraham, let me tell you how the system works. If a white boy gets caught dealing drugs, his rich daddy will hire a lawyer. His son will be out of jail within an hour. His record will be clean in two hours. This will cost about five thousand dollars. If you get arrested, you will stay in jail for months. I don't have five thousand dollars or a lawyer. DO YOU UNDERSTAND THAT! YOUNG MAN, IT AIN'T FAIR! IT AIN'T FAIR. IT AIN'T FAIR! BUT THAT IS HOW IT WORKS!"

I stood up, stormed out of the kitchen, and ran out of the apartment. I had to be alone. I was angry. I had to think things out and calm down. As I walked down the street, I saw Dee heading in my direction. I waved, and he waved back. He was walking with two gang members. They were just walking and laughing. Then, out of nowhere, two men wearing jogging clothes ran past me and then past them. Suddenly, I saw the hand-off. It was quick. It was smooth. Then, just as quick and just as smooth, the two men turned and showed their badges. Dee and his two friends were put in the back of a patrol car and taken away. Their life was over. They would now have a record.

I was less than a block away. In just two more minutes, I would have been talking with them. In just two more minutes, I would have been in the back seat of that police car. I FROZE. I watched it all happen. I watched as Dee looked out of the police car window at me as he passed. His expression said it all. His life had suddenly changed.

I was lucky. I was extremely lucky. I now understood what Grandma was telling me, "A boy in the projects doesn't have a chance." Two minutes, just two minutes could have changed my life. I turned around and walked back to my apartment. I walked into the kitchen and saw Grandma still sitting at the kitchen table. She was praying. I walked over to her and quietly sat in the chair next to her. She stopped praying. I laid my head on her shoulder. I didn't say anything. Grandma could feel my pain. Then I said, "They just arrested Dee."

Then I hugged Grandma. I told her I was sorry for what I said, and I was afraid. I told her I didn't know what I was going to do. I told Grandma I felt like a caged animal. All my friends were in gangs. If we moved, it won't be any better. Plus, we didn't have any money, so how could we move? I hugged Grandma, and she hugged me. We sat there for a long time. It was a long night. The next morning, Grandma told me to stay home from school. She told me it wouldn't be safe for me to be at school today.

I assumed Dee would be going to school. I also knew that he saw me when he was arrested. I sat on the sofa in the living room and waited. Dee and I usually walk to school together. I waited for Dee to knock on the door, but he never did. The living room was dark. I just sat there in the dark. Then I stood up and looked out the window. There was no sign of Dee. I jumped when the phone rang. Grandma answered it, then she said, "That was Dee on the phone. He's still in Juvie. He told me to tell you to be careful. Other gang members are looking for you."

I was trapped in my apartment. I couldn't go anywhere. I had to stay out of sight. I turned on the TV, then turned it back off. I went to my room and just lay on my bed. I stayed there all day. It was a long day full of nothingness.

Around three o'clock in the afternoon, after school let out, I started hearing voices of the students walking past our apartment coming home from school. I wanted so much to be one of them. Then there was a knock at the door. I carefully peeked out the window and saw a little girl standing at the door. I opened the door, but left the chain lock secure. She quickly handed me a note, then turned and ran away. I took the note into the kitchen and opened it. It read, "WE KILL RATS IN OUR NEIGHBORHOOD." I showed the note to

Grandma. Grandma sat down at the table. She just sat there staring at the note. Then she said, "Abraham, we have to be careful, and you have to be very careful. They are going to try to hurt you in order to hurt me. These are bad kids." I stood up and went to my room. I sat on the edge of the bed thinking about what Grandma said.

That was when I heard the sound of a car and beat of loud rap music. It was outside of our apartment. It wasn't making a normal car sound. It was too loud, and it wasn't moving. I went into the living room and carefully peeked out the window from behind the curtains. The car was full of boys, and they were all looking at my apartment. Then the car slowly started moving toward the end of the block. It stopped and turned around. I watched as the car lights blinked twice. That was when I knew what was going to happen. Two blinks are the sign of a DRIVE-BY!

I yelled out to Grandma, "**GET ON THE FLOOR, DRIVE-BY! DRIVE-BY!**" Then I hit the floor and listened as the car moved toward our apartment. The sound of rap music kept getting louder and louder. Then I heard bullets hitting the apartment building, lots of bullets. They shot out all the windows in our apartment. I crawled across the floor and back to the kitchen. Grandma was on the floor, praying. I crawled over next to her and held on to her. We stayed there all night. No one came to help us. The police didn't come. The neighbors didn't come. NO ONE CAME! I think everyone was afraid to come. We were totally alone.

The next day was strange. First, I woke up on the kitchen floor, not in my bed. Next, Grandma suggested that I not go to school again today. At first, I was excited to stay home from school, but I also wanted to go to school. I wanted to be with my friends. I told Grandma that I'd be careful.

That was when she told me, "No Abraham, I have a plan. You need to listen. Little A, if you stay here, they are going to kill you. I should not have helped Mr. Lang. I think they are going to kill you in order to punish me. You have to leave. You have to go someplace where they can't find you. It won't be for long, but you have to leave for a short time."

Again, I asked Grandma, "But where? They know where I go to school. I can't stay inside all day. Where would I go?"

Grandma was very calm. She stared at me and said, "I don't know, Abraham. Let's pray about it." Then she reached over and held my hand. I didn't know what to say. I just sat there and watched as Grandma started praying. Then she suddenly stopped and looked up at me. "Abraham, aren't you going to pray with me?"

I told Grandma that I would pray, but this wasn't a God thing. This was a ---. Then I stopped talking! The expression on Grandma's face changed. It was a look of shock, anger, sadness, and confusion.

She spoke to me in a voice of disbelief, "**NOT A GOD THING? ABRAHAM, EVERYTHING IS A GOD THING, EVERYTHING.**" Then the room went silent. I didn't know what to say, and Grandma was now in tears. She lowered her voice to almost a whisper. "Abraham, you and I go to church every Sunday. We pray every day. How can you say this is not a God thing? Abraham, either you believe or you don't."

I told Grandma that I believed in God, but I don't believe God did what people asked him to do. He had his own game plan.

Grandma held my hand a little tighter. She told me to pray with her. Then she started to pray, "**GOD, WE NEED HELP.**" That was her prayer. That was all she said. She looked up at me and said, "Abraham, I don't tell God what to do, I just tell him what my problems are and ask Him to hold my hand."

On that day, sitting in the kitchen with Grandma, I learned how to pray. When Grandma said that, my hand began to shake. I reached over with my other hand, and it began to shake. Then I heard someone knocking on the front door. It was a loud knocking sound, and it didn't stop. It sounded like the police, but it wasn't. It was a tall Black man wearing a dark suit and pastor's collar.

His voice was deep, yet soft. He asked, "Are you Abraham?"

"Yes sir," was all I could say.

He smiled and said, "Then your grandmother must be my sister, Clara May." When he said that, I could hear Grandma scream out loud. She ran to the door like God Almighty was standing there. She grabbed the man and started yelling, "Eliza, Eliza, Eliza!" Then she dragged him inside and introduced me to her youngest brother. I didn't even know she had any brothers still alive. He told us that he was a missionary and lived in Africa. Grandma told him she thought he was dead. When Grandma said that, Eliza started laughing. "Well, Clara May, I was dead for a long time. I was spiritually dead. Then something happened that woke me up from the dead."

I had to ask, "What woke you up?"

He looked down at me and said, "An elephant!"

"AN ELEPHANT?" I shouted!

"Yes, young man. An elephant stepped on me and told me to stop drinking and doing drugs. I promised God that if He would let me live, I would stop drinking and join His army. And here I am. AMEN!"

I looked over at Grandma and asked, "Grandma, what did you pray for?"

She smiled and said, "Abraham, I prayed for help."

It turned out that her brother had been sent to Memphis to raise funds to support an African ministry. He was sent because he was the only missionary who could speak English. He told us he was staying with a family on the other side of town. He just arrived two days ago and wanted to surprise Grandma, and he succeeded!

Grandma, Eliza, and I sat at the kitchen table. Grandma still had tears of joy rolling down her face. Then Eliza told us that the family he was staying with had a boy about my age, his name was Jacob.

Grandma and Eliza talked non-stop all afternoon. Grandma couldn't believe that Eliza was still alive. He told us that during his bad times he spent most of his time in an African prison. There were no phones or anyway for him to tell Grandma that he was still alive. He said that the gangs in Africa ruled the country, and were cruel to prisoners. That was when Grandma told Eliza about our situation.

Eliza got up from the table and made a phone call to the family he was staying with. He returned to the kitchen and said, "Abraham, if it is okay with your grandmother, you can come with me until things start getting better.

You can stay with the family who is sponsoring my ministry to America."

Grandma looked over at me. "Abraham, this is the answer to my prayer. You have to go. I promise, it will only be for a short time, but you have to go. You can't stay here another day. Do you understand?"

Grandma and I had never argued before. She was talking and crying at the same time. I knew she didn't want me to leave. I also knew she was right. So, all I said was, "Yes, Grandma."

Grandma stood up and told me to quickly pack my stuff. I tossed some stuff into a suitcase and followed Eliza and Grandma out the front door. Eliza told me to get into the car. Grandma looked sad. She grabbed and hugged me so tight I couldn't breathe. Then she let go of me and gently pushed me inside the car. She slammed the door behind me. Then Eliza made a speedy exit out of the apartment complex.

I was on my way to a neighborhood on the other side of Memphis. Everything happened so fast I didn't have time to even think about where I was going. All I knew was, I was on a new journey.

The Journey

The journey started with me looking out the back window of Eliza's car. Grandma was standing with her arms wrapped around herself. I knew she wanted me out of danger. However, I was moving from Binghampton to a white town and a rich town. I had heard about East Memphis, but never thought I would ever live there. It wasn't that far from where I lived, but it was totally different. It was an old part of Memphis. The streets were full of big houses and expensive cars. It was a place where people in Binghampton went to work as maids and yard men during the day and return home at 4PM.

The truth was, I didn't want to leave Grandma or Binghampton. I knew it was dangerous, but Binghampton was my home. That was where my friends lived. That was where I looked like everyone else. I knew every person in my apartment complex, and they knew me. It was where I belonged. But no one asked me if I wanted to leave. Grandma told me to leave, and I was now on my way to a new home.

I felt awful. For the first time in my life, I felt abandoned. I felt scared. I felt angry. I felt homesick. The only good thing about the journey was Eliza and his laughter. When he laughed, his whole body laughed. And that made me laugh.

As Eliza drove down Poplar Avenue, I looked out the window and watched my neighborhood as it passed by. As we passed the 7/11 store, at the corner of Tillman and Walnut Grove, I started laughing. I remembered the crazy old man and Grandma with her iron skillet. It caused me to laugh out loud. Eliza looked over at me and said, "Young man, you have a great laugh. What's so funny?"

I told Eliza that last year I was walking home from school with my friends. We always went by the 7/11 store, the one we just passed. A group of old men were sitting out front telling stories and drinking beer. As I started to go in the front door of the store, one of the old men grabbed me and tried to kiss me. Then he started talking trash. I kicked him in the leg and ran like Hell.

When I got home, Grandma knew something was wrong. Grandma and I talk about everything. I told her about the old man. When I told her, she went into her closet and picked out one of her huge purses. Then she went to the kitchen and picked out one of her large iron skillets. She put the skillet inside her purse. Then she asked me to take her back to the store and show her the man who grabbed me. While Grandma was talking, she was walking toward the front door at full speed. She told me to hurry.

I was having a hard time keeping up with an old lady and her cane. It wasn't long before we reached the store. Grandma asked, "Abraham, which man grabbed you?"

I pointed to one of the men. She told me to stay where I was. Then she walked over to where the men were sitting. She pointed to the man who grabbed me. She asked, "Did you grab my grandson?"

He started to laugh. He looked at Grandma and said, "So what? What are you going to do old lady, hit me with your damn purse?" Then he turned and faced his friends while laughing. This was a BIG mistake on his part. Soon all the old men started to laugh. While the dirty old man was facing his friends, Grandma walked over and hit him on the back of his head with her iron skillet purse. It sounded like a baseball bat hitting a homerun. He dropped to the ground like a rock.

I told Eliza, "Then Grandma turned around, and we just walked away. I could hear the men laughing for blocks. I followed Grandma back to the apartment. She never said a word, but I was impressed. We had Spam and rice for dinner that night. During dinner I looked over at Grandma, and she looked back at me. She winked and told me to never underestimate the power of the Lord. I laughed, she laughed."

When I finished my story, Eliza laughed and applauded. I smiled and took a bow from the front seat of his car. It was the beginning of a new journey. It was also the beginning of a new friendship.

My New friend, Jacob

When I stepped out of Eliza's car, I was greeted by a very large white man. His name was Rev. Morton. He was wearing a dark blue suit, a pastor's collar, and a smile that made me feel like I was welcomed. He said, "Welcome Little A, or do I call you Abraham?"

I told him, "I preferred Little A. Grandma was the only person who ever called me Abraham."

He reached out, shook my hand, and then he grabbed me into a huge bear hug, just like Grandma. He asked me to join him and his son, Jacob. They were on their way over to his church. I walked over to his car, a new BMW. His son, Jacob, was sitting in the front seat. Jacob looked very much like me, only he was white. When I got into the car, Jacob didn't look very happy. There was a problem, and I wondered if the problem had my name on it.

Jacob didn't say a word. He just sat there in the front seat looking straight ahead. He didn't say hello. He just sat there. When Rev. Morton got in the car, he turned around and looked at me. He said, "I've been looking forward to meeting you. If you like basketball, you and Jacob should have a lot of fun together."

Jacob still didn't say a word. He just sat there looking out through the windshield. Rev. Morton looked over at Jacob and asked, "Are you going to say something or not?" Jacob said, "At least he's sitting in the back of the bus."

Rev. Morton rolled his eyes and gave me a look that said, "I'm Sorry." Then he looked over at Jacob and said, "THAT, YOUNG MAN, WAS NOT CALLED FOR!"

I just sat in the back seat and said nothing. I didn't know what to say, but Rev. Morton knew what to say. And he was not a happy camper. He started the car and drove over to his church. When we arrived, he got out and told both of us to follow him. His voice was now deeper and more commanding. Jacob and I walked into the church following Rev. Morton. Jacob's expression had changed. I could tell he knew something I didn't know.

We went into the chapel. Rev. Morton stood there, looked around the room, then said, "Boys, this place needs cleaning." When he said that, Jacob looked over at me and rolled his eyes.

Rev. Morton took us to the back closet where all the cleaning supplies were kept. Then he said, "You two boys need to get to know each other, and you need to do it on your own. I'm not going to lecture to you or tell you how to be friends. You two boys will just have to figure it out on your own. And while you are doing that, you can clean the chapel area of the church. Jacob knows how to do it. I'll be back in about an hour. If I don't see a clean chapel, I'll give you another hour." Then Rev. Morton turned and walked out of the church. He slammed the door on his way out. Jacob looked at me, and I looked at him. Then Jacob started laughing.

He handed me a dusting rag and some cleaner. He continued laughing and said, "Welcome to my world, Little A." I asked him what he wanted me to do. He gave me a sharp look and said, "Frankly, I want you to go home."

I told him, "I want to go home to, but my Grandma insisted I leave. She insisted I live where I would be safe. Gangs are looking for me back home. But if you don't want me here, then I'll leave."

Then I laid my cleaning supplies on a church pew, turned, and walked out the front door of the chapel. I didn't know where to go, but I just kept walking. I was about a block away from the church when I heard Jacob call for me to stop. He was running at full speed to catch me. When he caught up with me, he was out of breath, but he managed to say, "Little A, I'm sorry, don't leave. If you leave, my dad will make me clean the whole damn church, sweep the parking lot, and wash his car. Then he started laughing again. "Little A, I was wrong, okay. Let's go back and finish cleaning the chapel before Dad returns? And, while we're cleaning, tell me about the gangs. Are they really after you?"

As we headed back to the church, I replied, "Yes. The gangs are after me. It's a long story. I'll tell you everything while we're cleaning."

That was the beginning of our friendship. Jacob didn't know me, and I didn't know him. He didn't know Black, and I didn't know white. Rev. Morton was a smart man. He knew that friendships couldn't be forced. He knew that Jacob and I had to build our own friendship, or it wouldn't work.

As Jacob and I cleaned the church, we talked about a lot of stuff. Over the next hour, Jacob learned about my world, and I learned about his. I wasn't surprised to learn that he had his own issues. I learned that white kids in big houses have the same problems growing up as Black kids in small apartments. Maybe they even have more problems. Maybe having too much is worse than having too little.

In less than an hour, we were friends not enemies. Rev. Morton was right. We had to build our friendship on our own terms. Jacob really did become like my brother. Over time we shared stories that only brothers would share. I learned about where and how he lived, and he learned about the inner city of Memphis, where I lived. We were both shocked that there was such a difference between the way we each saw the other person. Jacob thought that the inner city of Memphis was all poor Black people who didn't want to work and didn't have the intelligence to achieve. He called us underachievers and lazy.

I told Jacob that wasn't true. I told him there were lots of smart people in the inner city. I also told him that I made all A's in school. When I asked him what his grades were, he laughed and said, "I'd rather not talk about grades." We listened to each other. We didn't argue. We learned from each other, and we both changed. I wondered why adults didn't do the same thing. Grandma was right. I had to move. I had to get away from some bad gangs. Plus, I now had an opportunity to experience what life was like outside the invisible wall around Binghampton.

My Temporary New Home

Jacob's family was different from what I had expected. His father was a minister, and they lived in a very nice house. Plus, Rev. Morton drove a BMW. But something was wrong.

Rev. Morton was a large man, and a true man of God. He was love on two legs. His wife, Kierra, was a small lady. She was nice, but she also had a hard side. I knew right off she was the boss! She was like Grandma. She was soft and motherly, but she also had a hard side. However, even with her hard side, she was unable to control Jacob. Jacob, I discovered, was not the perfect son.

During dinner, on my first night, I observed their rocky relationship. I could tell that Ms. Kierra knew Jacob was, once again, in trouble. She didn't say anything, but I saw the expression on her face. I also saw the way she watched me, as if I were guilty of something. I heard the words she didn't say. Grandma used to tell me that she could hear the words I didn't say. Now I understood what she meant. Dinner was quiet. There wasn't any laughter or conversation like, "How was your day, or tell me about your day."

It was pretty obvious to me that Jacob either belonged to a gang or was hanging with the wrong kids. He had an attitude. Jacob was easy to read. Ms. Kierra was also easy to read. She didn't take any ------ well, ----- any crap from Jacob. She was tough. She even scared me!

Jacob and I shared a bedroom. I could tell that Jacob wasn't happy about that arrangement. When boys don't like something, they usually say what's on their mind. I have always been up front about things with other people. So, when Jacob and I went to bed that night, and were alone, I told him I was sorry to have been dumped on him and his family. He told me that I wasn't the problem. He said he was the problem, but didn't want to talk about it. Our first night was both quiet and, for me, sleepless.

Our second night was anything but quiet. It was Wednesday night. Rev. Morton and Ms. Kierra were at church. Jacob and I stayed home to do our homework. My new school was very demanding. I had a lot of work to do just to catch up with everyone else. At my new school, everyone was an overachiever. I was afraid my grades were going to drop. I thought Jacob might help me, but I was wrong. He didn't even do his homework. After about an hour of doing my homework, I closed my books and asked

Jacob if we could talk. I told him what we said would not leave the room, but we had to be honest and up front with each other.

I started off with some tough questions, and Jacob tried to avoid my questions. Then he finally exploded! "STOP! STOP ASKING ME ABOUT GANGS AND STUFF. YOU KNOW. YOU KNOW GANGS ARE EVERYWHERE. WHAT DO YOU WANT ME TO SAY?"

I told Jacob, "You don't have to say anything. I already know. I know you wear the same color every day, red. I know you hang with the same boys. All the boys wear the color, red. And, today at school, it was obvious that the boys were divided into groups or gangs. Something was getting ready to go-down. It was exactly like that at my old school."

Then I told Jacob about my friends joining gangs and about the drive-by. He just laughed at me. He said, "Well, Little A, join the gang." Then he laughed and told me he was going to bed. That ended that conversation.

In the morning when I woke up, Jacob was already gone. Ms. Kierra told me he had a preschool meeting. I didn't say anything at first. Then I asked Ms. Kierra, "What kind of meeting starts before classes?"

This made Ms. Kierra angry. She said in a harsh voice, "LITTLE A, DON'T TELL ME HOW TO RUN MY FAMILY! You are welcome, but it's not your concern."

I told her that I would never tell her how to run her family, I just wanted to help. But she immediately said, "NO! I don't want your help. I also don't want my husband to know about Jacob."

Ms. Kierra just stood there, cold as ice. Then she told me to not tell her husband anything. She told me it wasn't a gang. It was more like a club. I told her, "NO, it's a gang. And the longer you ignore the truth, the harder it will be to break the bond between Jacob and the gang members."

Ms. Kierra said, "I can handle it. You have to stay out of it. If you can't, I will send you back to where you came from. Do you understand?"

All I said was, "Yes Ms. Kierra, I understand." When I said that, I could feel the room growing colder and colder and colder. The look on her face was one of pure anger. I knew, by her words and the way she looked at me, that something was wrong. I wasn't wanted. I knew my time with their family was over. Plus, I missed Grandma. I now understood what Grandma called "the badness" was everywhere. It wasn't just my neighborhood. It was all neighborhoods, rich and poor, Black and white.

That was the night I decided to leave. I talked with Eliza on the phone. I told him I had to leave. I asked him if he would take me home. His reply was unexpected. He said, "No, I can't take you home, not yet. Jacob needs you. He just doesn't know how much he needs you, but he does. And you only have a few days left to help him."

I was totally confused. "What are you talking about? What's going to happen to Jacob in a few days?"

"Little A, I have to leave. I cannot take you home, but Rev. Morton can. If you decide to leave and do nothing to help Jacob, soon Jacob will no longer be a problem. Jacob needs you. That is all I can tell you. The next time you blink your eyes, I'll be gone, and you will not remember this conversation. Good luck young man."

I shouted, "STOP, STOP! **WHO ARE YOU?** WHAT DO I DO?

All I heard before I blinked was, "Little A, I'm an Angel."

Then I blinked.

That night I waited for everyone to go to bed. Then I packed up my stuff and started to crawl out the bedroom window. As I started out the window, Jacob sat up and asked, "Little A, stop! Where ya going?"

I told him, "Back home, Jacob, back home. I think something bad is going to happen, and I can't stop it. I've got to go." That was when Jacob asked me to stop. He said, "Little A, you're right. Can we talk?"

I said, "Sure." Then I crawled back into the room and sat on the floor next to his bed. Jacob was different. He looked scared. He sat on the edge of his bed and said, "Little A, can I go with you? Little A, I need to go with you!"

I told Jacob, "Sure, but it isn't going to be easy. My neighborhood is not like yours. Are you sure you want to go?"

He replied, "Little A, I have to go with you! I'm in trouble. Tomorrow is not going to be a good day. That's all I can tell you."

Jacob jumped out of bed and packed his stuff into two sports bags. Then we climbed out the window and started the journey back to my home. I knew it was going to be a long night. Jacob and I started walking the entire way home. While we walked, we had to avoid the police. We made our way down Poplar Avenue, toward the inner city. It wasn't long before I saw a city bus coming in our direction. City busses didn't run that late at night. So, I took a chance and flagged it down. To my surprise, it stopped. The sign on the bus read, "Jesus."

When the door of the bus opened, I told the driver we didn't have any money. He laughed, "I know that Little A, get in." I asked the driver how he knew my name. He told me that he lived in Binghampton. He laughed and said, "Little A, everybody knows you."

So, Jacob and I got on the bus. The driver talked to us all the way back home. When we arrived at Tillman Street, he stopped. I didn't tell him to stop, he just stopped. Then he told us to be careful.

Jacob and I stepped off the bus into darkness, but I knew where I was. I also knew this was not a good place for us to be at that time of night. This entire block of Binghampton belonged to the gang that Grandma had made mad.

Jacob and I had to move fast. I had to find a new way to get to my apartment. I used back streets and allies to avoid being seen. I told Jacob to be quick and follow my lead. I also told him, if we got caught, he had to run and hide. They wanted me, not him. I no sooner said that then I saw the gang members. They were like roaches crawling out from under everything. They were everywhere. They just stepped out of the darkness and started moving in our direction. Jacob froze. I froze. I was too scared to move. Suddenly I saw the gang leader step out in front of everyone. He started laughing. "Little A, what tha' Hell are you doing out this late? You know it's not safe! And who is your new friend?"

I didn't know what to say. The gang didn't look angry or hostile. I replied, "This is my friend, Jacob. We're on our way home. We don't want any trouble."

Then the gang leader said, "I know. Your grandma asked me to meet you and make sure you got home safe."

I didn't understand. Was the gang leader going to walk with us to my apartment? Was he making sure we were safe? At first, I thought it was a trick. Then I realized he was serious. As we walked down Tillman, he talked about stuff as if we were old friends. I was totally confused. I kept waiting for something bad to happen, but nothing happened. When we got to my apartment, Grandma was waiting for me on the front steps. She stood up and said, "Thanks, Louis."

NOW I WAS REALLY CONFUSED. WHY WAS GRANDMA THANKING LOUIS, THE HEAD GANG MEMBER? I walked over to Grandma and gave her huge hug. When I did that, Grandma reached over and pulled Jacob into the hug. She said, "I missed you, Abraham. I am glad you are home, and I am glad to see Jacob. Things are now going to be just fine."

I stood there totally confused. I asked Grandma, "What's going on? Why did Louis walk us home and not beat us up? Grandma, what did you do? Did you pay him to walk us home?"

Grandma laughed and said, "No. I didn't pay him. I just made him some cookies, that's all. That's all I did, make cookies." Then Grandma told Jacob and me to pick up our stuff and come inside. She also told Jacob to call his parents and let them know where he was and that he was okay.

As I walked through the front door of our apartment, I smelled cookies. I looked over at Grandma. She had a big grin on her face. "Okay," I asked, "what's going on."

Then I walked into the kitchen. The kitchen shelves were full of glass jars. And inside all the jars were cookies. And on the outside of every jar was the name of a gang member. I sat down at the kitchen table and looked over at Grandma. "Grandma, I think we need to talk." Grandma sat down at the table and started telling me about the cookie jar project.

She told me that she missed me. She needed someone to look after, so she decided to adopt all the boys on the street, gang boys. Only Grandma would think of something that simple, that crazy, and it worked. A few weeks after I left town, Grandma made some cookies. Then she put them in jars and went over to Tillman Street. It wasn't long before one of the gang members approached her. Grandma handed him a jar full of cookies and told him to put his name on the outside. Then she told him when the jar was empty, to put the empty jar on her back stoop. She told him she would then put more cookies in the jar for him. She also told him that she would put cookies in any jar placed on her back stoop. This became so popular, she started keeping the jars in her kitchen, with a note on the back door telling the boys to come in and get their cookies. She started leaving the back door unlocked. Boys not only enjoyed her cookies, but they also started leaving her "thank you" notes. Grandma pulled out a cardboard box from under the table. It was full of thank you notes. The notes were written on scrap pieces of paper, the word "LOVE" was on many notes. The gang boys now had a mother that loved them, and they loved her. I just sat there speechless.

Grandma laughed. She told me that she was the safest person in Binghampton. I looked over at Jacob and started laughing. Jacob didn't laugh. He didn't understand. He just sat there like we were all crazy, and I think we were. However, it was a wonderful type of crazy. Grandma did something no one in the city of Memphis could have done. She didn't put young boys in jail. She didn't sit back and say, "It's not my problem." She didn't say, "Let's organize a committee." Grandma just made cookies, lots of cookies. GO FIGURE. COOKIES!

The Goodness
Stories

Grandma was different, a wonderful kind of different. But I could see her getting older and weaker. The next morning was Saturday. When Jacob and I went into the kitchen to get her wonderful pancakes, Grandma wasn't there. I went to her bedroom, and she was still in bed. She was still asleep. She looked so comfortable, so happy. I didn't want to wake her up. I went to the kitchen and looked at all the cookie jars. Then I fixed Jacob and myself a bowl of cereal.

While we were eating our cereal, a boy walked in the back door, said "Good morning," and took down his jar of cookies. Then he sat at the table with us. Then another boy walked in, then another, and another. Before long, the kitchen was full of kids eating cookies and laughing.

Then Grandma walked in and gave every boy a hug, and they all hugged her. Grandma looked so happy, but she also looked tired. For the first time I could remember, she looked old. She still had on her nightgown and slippers. She looked at all the kids that filled her kitchen from wall to wall, and smiled from ear to ear. Then she said,

"Boys, it's a beautiful day. So, before you head off to play basketball, let's sit outside on the steps and eat cookies. Plus, now that Abraham is home, I want to tell you a story."

I sat there and watched Grandma treat every gang member as if each boy were her own grandson. I didn't understand what was taking place; but whatever it was, it was good. We all walked outside, like little boys in kindergarten, and sat on the ground waiting for Grandma's story. Then she started telling us a story I had never heard before. Grandma started in a low and quiet voice.

"Boys, I grew up in the country on a farm. Momma, Daddy, Eliza, and I all worked the farm. We worked six days a week, from sunup to sundown. My daddy died at the age of ninety-three. One day he didn't come home for lunch. We always had our big meal at lunchtime because it was too hot to work in the fields. So, Momma sent me out to get him. I walked over to the far end of the field and found Daddy lying on the ground behind his plow. Both his mules, Clyde and Homer, were standing next to him. He looked like he was resting and just fell asleep. He farmed over fifty acres with nothing more than two old mules and a hand-made plow. When I went over to wake him up, I realized Daddy was dead. Clyde and Homer seemed to know this. They just stood there.

I don't know how long they had been standing there, but it was as if they were paying their respects to my daddy. I think my daddy loved those old mules more than he loved my momma."

This caused a lot of laughter among all of us. And I think this was the first time I saw Jacob laugh, **really laugh**! He laughed so hard his sides hurt. Then Grandma continued.

"Daddy and those old mules worked as a team twelve hours a day, six days a week, sunup to sundown. When you spend that much time with a person or animal, you either love'm or hate'm. Daddy chose to love them. That was the day I went from helping Momma in the kitchen to plowing the fields. It was hard work, but it was also fun. Clyde and Homer became my best friends. When we weren't working the fields together, we were playing together. I rode Clyde everywhere. Homer always followed along just to be with us. After I grew up and started having kids, I had six boys. The first two were twins. I named them Clyde and Homer. I never told this story to my boys, but now you know."

Once again everybody started laughing, and this time they applauded! I sat there totally amazed. A week or two ago, these boys wanted to kill me (or anyone). Now they are all like family. Grandma had magic in her soul. It's called, **GRANDMOTHER'S LOVE.**

After her story, everyone headed down to the basketball courts. Grandma sat with Jacob and me on the back stoop. She hugged both of us again. "Little A, Jacob, you boys don't have no time to just be boys. Everybody wants to steal your childhood. It's not fair. You boys belong to me, not to nobody else."

That day, on the back stoop, was the beginning of many stories. I think Grandma knew something I didn't know. I think she wanted to tell me, or us, her stories before she died in the field behind her own Clyde and Homer.

At the time, I just didn't understand what I was seeing. Another thing I didn't understand were girls. I was twelve years old and it's called "Coming of Age." The next chapter you read is both funny and important. I knew I liked girls, but I didn't know the rules. I didn't even know there were rules. I only knew what other boys told me or what I saw on T.V., and none of that information was true. Believe me, **THERE ARE RULES, VERY IMPORTANT RULES ABOUT GIRLS!**

The Rules about Girls and (Coming of Age)

She was a new student at my school, and she was beautiful. When I went to school on Monday, she was sitting in the desk in front of me. I was at that age. I knew I was at that age. The hormones were beginning to flow, and I liked it. I was suddenly in love with a girl I'd never met. This sounds crazy, but love is crazy. And love starts at a very early age.

Did I tell you she was beautiful? I couldn't stop looking at her. Then, one day, she turned around and told me to stop staring at her. How did she know I was staring at her? However, I was. Her name was Brandi. Did I tell you she was beautiful?

When we got home from school, Grandma, Jacob, and I sat down at the kitchen table to talk. Grandma asked, "Well boys, how was school today?"

I smiled and said, "Grandma, it was great!" Then Jacob started laughing.

Grandma looked over at me, smiled, and asked, "Okay, what's her name?"

"Brandi. She sits in front of me in Math class. How did you know it was a girl thing?" Jacob started laughing. He joined in with, "Little A, everyone in the classroom knows. Everyone knows you're hot for Brandi, even Brandi knows."

I didn't understand how everyone knew how I felt. However, Jacob told me that I was acting different. He told me that I was teasing her, and she was teasing me. He said it was fun to watch.

Suddenly, I felt embarrassed. That was when Grandma asked Jacob and me, **"Boys, do we need to have the talk?"**

I quickly replied, **"NO, Grandma, NO! PLEASE!"**

But Jacob surprised me and said, **"Yes. I think we do need to talk."**

Then Grandma looked more like a teacher, not a grandma. She said, "Boys, there are rules that you need to know about girls. I can't make you follow the rules, but you need to know what the rules are, okay?"

I just sat there not knowing what Grandma was going to say. I was afraid she was going to say something about ---------------. **Then she said it!** "Boys, girls don't have peeeeenissss, and you do. So, you need to know the rules about boys and girls."

I looked over at Jacob and couldn't control myself. I replied, **"Peeeeenissss?"** Then I started laughing, Jacob started laughing, and then Grandma started laughing. After laughing so hard I could hardly talk. I was finally able to say, "Grandma, we know that."

Grandma looked at me and said, "Good. But there is a lot you don't know, and I am going to tell you."

Suddenly the room got quiet. Jacob and I stopped laughing. This talk was starting to get interesting. What could Grandma know that we didn't already know?

Grandma was serious, dead serious, and continued her lesson about boys and girls. "God created you to fall in love, and he created girls to fall in love. This is all good. But this does not mean you own a girl. Always treat a girl with respect. And know that what you call love is NOT what you read on bathroom walls or see in dirty magazines. Love, at your age, is a very special friendship. BUT IT IS NOT LIKE MARRIAGE. Do you know what I mean when I say it is not like marriage?"

I didn't know how to answer that question, but Jacob did. "You mean we can't have sex." I looked over at Jacob. I couldn't believe he said the word "sex"!

"CORRECT!" Grandma looked over at Jacob. "Jacob, you and I are going to get along fine. You say what you mean. I like that. Yes, you two boys need to know the truth, not what someone tells you. So, here's the truth.

"Sex is great and important. Without sex, we wouldn't have children. However, if you have sex at your age, you are killing your future. I don't care what anyone tells you, sex equals children. And it's not just the girl problem. You are also a part of the problem. Once you have a baby, you have to support the child. It's the law. **YOUR LIFE, AS YOU KNOW IT, IS OVER.** You will have to give up basketball and get a job, probably a crappy job. One time with a girl is all it takes boys, **JUST ONE TIME.** When you are with a girl, and things get a little hot, you have to be the one to say, 'NO, NOT NOW!'

"Boys think about it. Think about it long and hard. This is one thing that, if you choose to do it, will change your life forever. This is why I want you to know the truth. Sex was designed by God to be enjoyed, but you MUST wait for the right time. And the right time is <u>after you finish your education and after you have a good job.</u> And I hope it is <u>after you and your girlfriend agree to stay together and support your children.</u> Do you understand?"

I just sat there. I didn't know how to answer Grandma's question. So, I asked her a question. "Grandma, what if the girl wants to have sex? What if she tells me that if I don't, she will dump me for another boy?"

Grandma smiled. "Great question. If a girl says that, then you know it's not love. You know you have the wrong girl. The girl wants something. However, it's not love! This is when **you** have to be in charge of yourself and your actions. This is when you have to say, 'NO.' If she argues, she is not the girl for you. She is putting herself ahead of you. It isn't easy. But it's what you have to do!!

"Remember, education comes first. Education allows you to get a good job making a good salary. A good job comes next. A good job should be a career, not flipping burgers. Marriage can come at any time along the way, as long as you can afford to provide for your wife and children. Then you and your wife can enjoy sex the way God designed it. This is the way it's supposed to be, **NOT** what you see on TV."

Jacob said, "Ms. G, I hear you, but that is not the way it works today. That is the way it was when you were our age, but things have changed. Girls expect more than a kiss."

Grandma looked over at Jacob, "Jacob, do girls expect it or do **YOU** expect it?"

Jacob got quiet, then he said, "Ms. G, I hear you, but you don't understand."

"Jacob," Grandma interrupted, "Tell me what I don't understand."

Once again Jacob got quiet and thought about a good reply. Then he said, "Ms. G, things are just different now than when you were our age. That's a fact."

Grandma smiled and said, "You are right. Things are different now. You are absolutely right. This makes it much harder for you and Abraham to do what is right and NOT what other people tell you to do. So, here is an idea. When someone tells you it is okay to do something, look at the person who is giving you advice. How old are they? Are they more educated than you? Are they smarter than you? Or are they using you? **NEVER ALLOW SOMEONE ELSE TO CONTROL WHAT YOU DO**, unless they have earned that right, like a doctor or teacher or parent. Let me give you an example. At your age, you are old enough to own who you are. Don't give yourself away for other people to tell you what to do with your life. Children usually do what they are told to do. **You are no longer a child.** You must know who to trust, and that person just might not be your best friend or girlfriend.

"You know what is right and wrong. **Believe in yourself. Don't give your life away to another person.** If you allow other people to make your decisions, shame on you. If you do, you have just given yourself away."

When Grandma said that, the room got quiet. She was right. Jacob and I knew she was right. However, we both had a lot of peer pressure to be a part of what we thought was okay, normal, everyone's doing it, etc. We also saw stuff on TV all the time. Plus, we both had girlfriends.

I think that talk, on that day, was one of the most important talks I ever had with Grandma. I never forgot it. AFTER THAT TALK, I NEVER LET ANYONE CONTROL MY LIFE, MY RULES. At first it was hard for me to understand, but at least we had the talk. Knowing what is right or wrong, and doing what is right, isn't always easy. But it is an important part of growing up. Sometimes, growing up isn't easy. Growing up requires a person to make the right decision at the right time.

I never thanked Grandma for all her advice. I feel bad about that. She made growing up so much easier. Jacob and I are both who we are today because of who she was then. Why don't all parents talk to their boys about such an important topic? The TV and movies are selling sex to make money. Growing up is real. Hormones are real. Feelings are real. Plus, bad decisions are both real and irreversible.

The Return Home

Over the rest of the school year, everything pretty much went back to normal, whatever normal was for a twelve-year-old boy back then. However, Jacob never adjusted to the inner city way of living. I think he missed his big house and private bathroom. Plus, he missed his mom and dad and his old friends. So, at the end of the school year, he decided to return home. Rev. Morton and his wife welcomed Jacob back home. They immediately drove over to pick him up. I could tell that things were now much better between Jacob and his parents. Grandma did her magic on Jacob, and he was a different boy when he got into the car to go home. He now knew what it was like to live in the projects.

After Jacob returned home, Grandma got a call from Rev. Morton. He told Grandma that Jacob was a different kid. He said that Jacob was actually fun to be with. He thanked Grandma. Grandma laughed. I could see the pride in her face. I could also see tears start to fill her eyes. She missed Jacob.

It was about a week after Jacob left before I noticed his jar was gone. Jacob's cookie jar was missing. Go figure. Grandma removed the badness from boys one cookie at a time.

She Was, "Beautiful"

It was early, real early, on Saturday morning. I was still asleep when I heard someone knocking on the front door. I thought it was Dee or another one of my friends who wanted to play basketball. I ran to the door and opened it. There, standing in front of me, was a beautiful girl wearing a mailman's uniform. She had light brown skin, cornrows just like mine, freckles all over her face, and a smile from ear to ear. I was standing there wearing just my boxers. I wasn't expecting a girl to be at the door.

She said, "Here, I have something for your Grandma."

I quickly covered my boxers with both hands and asked, "Who are you?"

She smiled and replied, "I'm Beautiful."

I couldn't help but laugh. "I know that. I meant, what's your name?"

"Beautiful," is all she said.

I totally forgot about standing there in my boxers and asked, "Your name is Beautiful?"

She laughed and said, "Thank you. I like your name also. Abraham is a powerful name."

I tried to stop laughing but couldn't. "I meant, is your name Beautiful?"

She replied, "Yes. That is my God-given name, Beautiful."

"Where do you live? I've never seen you around here before. Are you new in the neighborhood?"

"Yes," she replied. Then she said, "Little A, you are getting taller." She reminded me to give the letter to my grandmother. Then she winked at me, turned, and walked back to her bicycle. She jumped on her bike and rode down the sidewalk and out of sight. I just stood there. That was the weirdest thing I had ever seen, and also the most beautiful. I was in love again. I was in love with a beautiful girl named Beautiful.

In a few minutes, Grandma walked up behind me and asked, "Who was that?" I laughed and told Grandma, "That is my new girlfriend." Then I handed the letter to Grandma. She looked at it and said, "Oh no!" Then she sat down on the sofa and just stared at the letter. It was special delivery. It was from someone in Society Hill, South Carolina. This was the town Grandma grew up in. It had to be bad news. Someone must have died. Grandma didn't want to open it. She just sat there with a strange look on her face. It was a look that told me she didn't want to know what was inside that envelope, a special delivery envelope from Society Hill, South Carolina. She slowly wiped her hands off on her apron and began to open the envelope, the special delivery envelope!

I stood there just watching Grandma. I didn't know what was in the envelope or how to respond to Grandma's reaction. She slowly opened up the letter and started reading it. That was when I saw her face change from sad to a look of excitement. Then she started to read the letter out loud.

"Dear Maggie, we are having a family/church reunion and want you to join us. The reunion would not be the same without you. We know times are hard. The attached check was donated from the Woman's Mission committee. We want you to come, and we hope you will join us on July 15th at the Missionary Baptist Church. The reunion will last all day, starting with the morning sermon. We will make arrangements for you to stay at the big house. Again, we hope you will join us. Please respond 'yes,' so we can make arrangements."

Grandma stopped reading. Her face was happy, really happy! She was happy and crying at the same time. I didn't know what to say or do. Then Grandma looked over at me and said, "Abraham, we are going home, my home. You are going to a place I call Goodnessville. You are going to meet the kindest people God ever created. You are going to meet my family, and your family. You've heard me tell you stories about growing up in a different time. Well, you are about to see for yourself what I was talking about. Abraham, we are going to Society Hill, South Carolina."

I asked Grandma, "Where is Society Hill, South Carolina?"

She told me to go to the library and look it up. So, the next day I went to the Memphis library and looked up Society Hill, South Carolina. It was located in the middle of South Carolina and in the middle of nowhere. It didn't look exciting, but I was looking forward to meeting my family. Grandma was so excited she sang hymns all day, every day. After two weeks of hymns, I was ready for the trip to begin.

Our trip started on Saturday morning. A friend of Grandma's took us to the bus terminal. It was a big bus with lots of people going everywhere. As I stepped onto the bus, I was surprised to see the person taking our tickets was the same girl who delivered Grandma's letter, Beautiful. This time, however, she was wearing a Greyhound Bus uniform. She smiled and said, "Little A, you and your grandmother have a great trip."

I looked at Beautiful. I was totally confused as to who she was or why she was taking my ticket. I sat in my seat and watched as Beautiful checked all the passengers. Then she walked past me, down the aisle, and off the bus.

This was just too weird. Who was this beautiful girl I had fallen in love with? I had a lot to learn about Beautiful. I also had no idea how much I was about to learn about myself.

The Angel

It was an early Sunday morning when the bus rolled into Society Hill, South Carolina. I looked out of the window and saw the WELCOME TO SOCIETY HILL sign roll by. In just a few minutes, the bus pulled off the road and into the parking lot of the Missionary Baptist Church. It wasn't a paved parking lot. It was more like driving across the church lawn. It was crazy, but it was home. When the bus stopped, Grandma and I stepped off into a sea of family. Everybody grabbed Grandma and hugged her until I thought she was going to die of happiness. I just stood there next to the bus. No one knew who I was. I was like a surprise package. I just stood there and watched and waited.

It was amazing. I never knew Grandma had such a large family. While I was standing there, I suddenly saw the girl again, the mail lady, Beautiful. She was standing a long way away, next to the church front door. But I knew it was her, and I waved. She saw me and waved back. Then she was gone. I ran over to the church, but she wasn't there. I looked everywhere, but she was gone.

Then Grandma called for me to come over and meet everyone. Everyone was glad to see me. After the adults

103

asked the usual adult questions: how old are you? What grade are you in? Etc. Some of the boys pulled me away from the adults. We shot baskets on the dirt court next to the church before church started. As soon as the church bells started to ring, the boys dropped the ball and headed to the church. Grandma motioned for me to join her for the service. I noticed that the boys just dropped the ball on the court and expected it to be there after church, (and it was). Grandma was right, this was going to be a new adventure.

When church was over, everyone went outside for lunch on the church lawn. I had never seen so much food and so much <u>good</u> food. While eating a plate full of fried chicken, I looked up and there she was again.

It was Beautiful. She was swinging on the swings, not eating with everyone else. I quickly took my plate and ran over to where she was swinging. She stopped swinging and took a piece of my chicken. She ate it and then took another piece. Then she laughed and said, "Best fried chicken I've ever had."

This time I wasn't going to let Beautiful get away without telling me who she was. It turned out to be easier than I thought. I just asking her, "Beautiful, who are you?"

She didn't say anything for a long time. She just continued eating my fried chicken. Then she whispered, "I'm an Angel."

I quickly replied, **"AN ANGEL?"**

She just smiled, "Yes, I'm an Angel, or an Angel in training."

I told her I didn't understand. I didn't think anyone could see an Angel.

She replied, "I think you're right. You're not supposed to see Angels, but for some reason you can see me. I don't know why. I'm new at this. I'm on my first assignment and not real sure of what I'm doing."

I asked her, "Is that why you have such an unusual name, Beautiful?"

"Yes. It is the name God gave me. My real name is Kunda."

I asked, "So, what do I call you, Beautiful or Kunda?"

She laughed. "I like Beautiful. I think it's a pretty name. After all, it's the name God gave me."

I just stood there for a long time trying to understand what was going on. Then I replied, "I don't understand. How can I see you if I am not supposed to see you?"

Beautiful replied, "I can't tell you why. Maybe because I'm not a full Angel yet. I'm just in training. There is a lot I don't understand about being an Angel."

I asked Beautiful, "How many Angels are there?"

She replied, "Lots!"

"Are they like you?"

"No. We are all different. Once a person becomes a full Angel, they don't know that they are Angels."

I quickly responded, "NO WAY."

Beautiful just looked at me, "Yes. Your grandmother changed Jacob, remember? When he went home, he was a different person."

I asked Beautiful, "Is Grandma an Angel?"

Beautiful, once again, started to laugh, "Sorry, can't tell you that. I shouldn't have told you about Jacob."

I asked, "What do you do all day, just fly around and watch people?"

Beautiful corrected me. "First, Angels don't fly, and we don't have wings. I don't know where all that information came from. However, we all have one mark that tells everyone we are Angels."

I asked, "What kind of mark?"

Beautiful just smiled. "Sorry, that's an Angel secret."

Just then I heard Grandma calling for me to come back to the table and finish eating. I returned to the table and everyone wanted to talk to me. Everyone wanted to know about life in the big city of Memphis. I told them a few things, but not the bad stuff. I was sitting at a large table with the kindest people I'd ever known. I didn't want bad words to ruin this group of friends and family. It was exactly as I had heard Grandma talk about. I was sitting at a table in a town Grandma called Goodnessville. I didn't want to say anything that would change those people. They didn't need to know about Binghampton, Gilbert, or PIT BULL.

It wasn't long before the boys pulled me away from the table full of adults. There must have been over twelve boys my age, and they were ALL going fishing and swimming. The first thing I noticed was no one wore shoes, so I stopped and took off my socks and shoes. The hot South Carolina sand under my feet felt great. We walked and told stories and sang stupid songs all the way to the pond, a very large pond. The boys stripped down to the skin and jumped off a high rock that overlooked the pond. I was quick to follow. We swam and fished the entire afternoon. We all talked and laughed at the same time. I think it was one of the happiest days of my life. It was so good that I began to wonder if it were too good. Was Beautiful here because of me? Was I dead and didn't know it? I knew there had to be an Angel somewhere, but where and why?

Around six o'clock, one of the men came down to get us, along with the fish we had caught. He drove an old red farm tractor pulling a hay trailer that was just as old. We all climbed aboard the hay wagon and headed over to what everyone called the Big House, and it was big! NO, it was **HUGE**. It was white, HUGE, three stories tall, with a large porch that wrapped around the entire house. As I rode in the hay wagon and came down the driveway toward this mansion of a house, I couldn't believe what I was seeing. The house was so big, so large, and so full of people. Plus, there were, once again, large tables outside, and all were full of food.

When the tractor stopped, everyone jumped off and ran to join their families who were already sitting at the tables. I saw Grandma. She was looking for me, and I was glad to see her. I was full of laughter and exhaustion. I was so tired I couldn't eat. I could feel my head almost dropping into my plate. Grandma kept talking to everyone. I had never before seen her that happy. She knew I was exhausted and rubbed my back to try and keep me awake.

After supper there was music, dancing, and singing. However, it had been a very long day, and I was exhausted. One of the boys showed me where the boys slept. The boys slept on the right side of the house on a large screened porch, and the girls slept on the left side of the house. I tried to stay awake but couldn't. I found a cot, laid down, and was asleep before knew I was asleep.

In the morning, the porch was full of boys. They were everywhere. They were on cots and on the floor. It was wall-to-wall boys. The first thing I remembered was the smell of pancakes, bacon, and coffee. Someone had placed a quilt over me during the night. I wanted to get up and eat breakfast, but I was too tired to move. Then I could hear other boys getting up. They were starting to talk and laugh. Then they all went down to the woods for their morning pee. Eventually I also got up, went to the woods, and then to breakfast.

Grandma was in the kitchen cooking for the entire group. There must have been fifty people in the house. Grandma just kept on cooking, so I went over to help her. She would cook, and I would serve it up. We made a great team. I even sang a few hymns with her. Everyone applauded her food and our singing. I could tell this was going to be another great day. Then, while serving food, I saw Beautiful looking through the window. I rushed outside to find her. She was sitting on the porch swing, slowly swinging back and forth.

I walked over and jumped on the swing next to her. I started talking about all the fun I was having, then I realized she wasn't saying anything. I looked over at her and asked, "What's wrong?"

All she said was, "Nothing."

I stared at her and said, "Beautiful, Angels don't lie very well. So, tell me what's wrong?"

She looked down, and not at me, "Little A, there is something I haven't told you yet. I didn't want to scare you."

I stopped swinging and sat there silently waiting for her next words. But there were no words. There was only silence. I noticed a tear rolling down her cheek.

"Little A," she slowly said, "You know I'm not a full Angel yet. God sent me to find you for a purpose. I didn't know what my assignment was going to be until last night."

I waited for Beautiful to tell me her story, but she just stopped talking. I told her, "You can't stop now. I need to know why you're here. Is it Grandma? You brought me the letter to give to Grandma. Is something wrong with Grandma? Is something going to happen to Grandma? Please, I need to know, please!"

Beautiful replied in a whisper, "Little A, I have already told you too much. Plus, you are not supposed to see me, but you can. However, I think I can tell you that your grandmother is not my assignment."

I asked Beautiful, "Then, who is your assignment?"

She looked away and whispered, **"You."**

Suddenly, some boys rushed over and told me it was time to go swimming. I jumped off the swing and joined the boys as we rushed to the pond for a cold dip. Everyone shouted, "The last one in is a rotten egg." I was the last one in. But even worse, I was also the last one to see the alligator. I didn't know there were alligators in Society Hill. No one told me to watch out for alligators. However, I soon discovered there were gators, and they were BIG.

As I swam out toward the middle of the pond, I heard the first warning, "ALLIGATOR, ALLIGATOR, GET OUT, GET OUT!"

When I heard, "ALLIGATOR," I thought it was a joke. Then I saw everyone swimming over to the side of the pond. I looked around and realized I was the only one still in the pond. Or, maybe I should say, I was the only boy in the pond. There was someone else, Mr. Gator.

He saw me, and I saw him. He was low in the water and quickly moving toward his next meal. I tried to swim, but it's impossible to outswim an alligator! I tried, but it didn't work. He was so close I could smell his breath. He opened his mouth and started to attack. I was going to die! Then, I heard a cannon going off, not once or twice, but over and over and over.

Mr. Gator stopped, looked at me, and then rolled over onto his back and just floated in the water next to me. Blood was pouring out of his body. I turned and looked over to the side of the pond where the boys were standing. There, I saw Grandma and ROSCOE. She was holding him with both hands. Smoke was still oozing out of the long barrel. Grandma was standing like an army sergeant, surrounded by a group of boys. She called out, **"ARE YOU OKAY, ABRAHAM?"**

I turned and swam to the edge of the pond. All the boys stood frozen in fear and surprise. They just starred at Grandma and Roscoe. She looked at them and asked, "Haven't you boys seen a gun before?" Then she told everyone to put on their clothes and follow her back to the Big House, away from the sight of the dead gator. The boys couldn't move fast enough. While everyone else was running ahead of us, I asked Grandma why she was at the pond and with Roscoe?

Grandma looked over at me and said, "A girl came running to the house and told me to come quick. When she said that, I knew you were in trouble. I came as fast as I could. When I got to the pond, I saw the gator moving in your direction."

That afternoon, everyone was talking about me, the gator, Grandma, and Roscoe. Grandma was a hero. The stories got better and better every time they were told and retold. After a while, I left the room and went outside to sit on the porch. I needed some quiet time.

While sitting on the porch, I felt someone sitting next to me. I looked over, and there she was. She looked over at me and smiled.

I asked her, "Did you tell my grandma to come help me?"

Her answer was one word, "Yes."

I asked, "Is that why you are here?"

Her answer was still one word, "No."

I asked, "Why are you here?"

She sat quietly for a long time. Then tears filled her eyes. Then she said, "I was sent here to guide you home to heaven."

I said, "ME?"

Beautiful said, "Yes, the alligator should have killed you. I stopped it from happening. I changed life because I didn't want you to die. I told your Grandma to save you, and she did. What I did was actually wrong. I saved your life, but that one change will have many other changes attached to it. It also cost me my Angel promotion. I'm okay, but I have to wait for another time to earn my promotion. I am not allowed to change anything, so I will start my training all over again.

"Little A, you are more important to me than becoming a full Angel. I fell in love with you the first time we met on your front stoop, and I think you fell in love with me.

"Little A, a real Angel can love without falling in love. Now, I will return home alone. And, as for you, I want you to live a good life. It is my gift to you, don't waste it. I will see you again many years from now, but you won't remember me. In fact, the next time you blink your eyes, I'll be gone. You won't remember me, but I will never forget you."

I blinked.

I Blinked

Just like that, in the blink of an eye, Beautiful was gone. She wasn't just physically gone; she was gone out of my memory. I found myself sitting alone on the back porch steps thinking about the alligator, Grandma, and Roscoe. I had to laugh. Grandma and Roscoe made everyone laugh.

Then I heard someone tell me to get packed up, the bus would be here soon. I stood up and went to the side sleeping porch to pack up my stuff. I was alone. Everybody else was inside talking and telling Grandma good-bye. However, I felt like something was missing. I couldn't figure it out. I kept looking through my old suitcase. I looked around the porch. The problem was, I didn't know what I was looking for. I just felt like something was missing. What I didn't know was I was missing a memory.

Suddenly, I had a feeling I had never felt before. It was a feeling of extreme joy and happiness. It was as if I had just won the NBA championship. I started crying tears of joy and started jumping around with excitement. Grandma came out on the porch and hugged me. She knew. Somehow, she knew everything.

Grandma

When we returned to Memphis, it felt like the neighborhood storm had blown over. The gangs didn't bother us. Grandma had made peace with everyone. The years seemed to pass by one after another. Grandma began marking my height on the doorframe next to the kitchen. My growth spurt came late; but when it came, I started growing like a weed. Before I knew it, I was in my senior year of high school. College was just around the corner. I was on the track team in high school and loved to run. It turned out that track was my ticket to college, or track and my good grades.

It was early on a Saturday morning, really early! Someone was knocking on our front door. They wouldn't stop knocking, so I got up and went to the door. When I opened the door, there stood the most beautiful girl I had ever seen. She smiled and said, "Good morning, Little A."

I said, "Good morning, who are you?"

She just stared at me, like I was supposed to know her. Then she began to laugh. "My name is Beautiful. I've come to see your grandmother. May I come in?"

I said, "Sure." Then she walked past me, as if I wasn't even there. She sat on the sofa next to Grandma. They were holding hands and talking and laughing. Grandma looked so happy, so excited. Suddenly the room became very silent, so silent I could hear Grandma's heart beating. Then it stopped beating. Beautiful looked over at me and smiled. I suddenly remembered her!

Then I blinked.

Postscript

(Henry looked over at me. He asked, "Papa, was she dead? Was your grandma dead? Was Beautiful really an Angel?"

I looked down at Henry, sitting on the shop floor, "Yes and yes."

"Papa, that story kind of scared me. Can you really see Angels?"

I paused before answering. "Henry, there are things that we just can't explain or prove. This is one of those things. I would never lie to you. I can only tell you what I saw and heard. Now, be quiet and let me finish the story,")

After I blinked, I saw only Grandma on the sofa. She looked like she was sleeping, but she wasn't. Grandma was with the Lord. I called our pastor. After the pastor arrived, he had Grandma removed. He told me to come home with him. I asked him if I could stay at the apartment until tomorrow. He agreed, then he left. I think he knew I needed time alone.

After he left, I also left. I walked down Tillman Street. It wasn't long before one of the gang boys approached me. I told him that Grandma had gone home to be with the Lord. He stood motionless. The expression on his face was hard to read. I turned and started to walk away. Then I heard his voice. He whispered, 'Little A, stop.'

I stopped and waited. I didn't know what he was going to do. I was ready to run. Then he walked over and hugged me. YES, HE HUGGED ME! He said, 'I'm sorry, I'll tell my brothers.' Then he turned and walked away. I asked myself, where did all the badness go? What did Grandma do besides make cookies?

I returned to the apartment, an empty apartment. It was now an apartment void of life. Without Grandma, it was different. I couldn't eat any supper; I wasn't hungry. I went to bed, and I finally realized that Grandma was gone. I cried. I cried as hard as a person could cry. My life had changed. Grandma was not there to help me anymore. However, I was no longer a boy growing up. I was now a young man. And, next week, I was scheduled to be on campus, a freshman, at The University of Memphis.

Around midnight I heard someone coming in through the back door. I got up, picked up my baseball bat, and cautiously made my way to the kitchen. I stood there and watched as boy after boy after boy came into the apartment. They all had their jar, and inside every jar was a note to Grandma. They put their jars and notes on the kitchen shelf. I watched as over twenty boys put their jars on the shelf, looked over at me, then walked out the back door. I stood silently and watched.

("Henry, Grandma was loved by every boy who came through that door. Grandma was like a mom to every boy on Tillman Street. I could feel the love. I could see the love. Grandma, once again, had performed her magic, and her magic was love. And yes, Henry, I think she was also an Angel. At least, she was an Angel to me."

Henry looked up at me. All he said was, "Thanks Papa. That was a good story." Then he said, "Papa, you remind me of your grandma."

Henry's eyes were full of tears, and so were mine. He stood up and hugged me. Then I told him the best part of my story.)

The next day the Pastor came to pick me up. I was all packed and waiting on the front stoop. He pulled up in front of the apartment and said, "Little A, quick, get in the car.

I tossed my stuff in the back seat and jumped into the car. I thought something was bad wrong. However, I was wrong. As the Pastor drove around Binghampton, every street sign had a graffiti peace symbol spray painted over the street name. Thanks to Grandma, there are no more gangs in Binghapton.

The End

Shirley Nelson Kersey, Ph.D.

Readers of the books of fiction featuring Little A, a boy living in the projects of Memphis, are instantly aware that the writer is eminently qualified to focus on this young hero. Only a person who has taught in the inner city schools is able to create a fictional, yet realistic account of the life of a youngster struggling to find himself in this environment.

John Chipley, whom the boys fondly have dubbed Mr. Chip, taught in Memphis inner-city schools for over fifteen years. In retirement he offers weekly volunteer sessions that focus on encouraging boys to read. This is a lofty goal, for the boys live in homes and neighborhood environments not structured to develop reading skills or dreams of career advancement. Mr. Chip's goal surpasses development of reading ability to encourage the boys to enjoy this privilege.

Chipley is formally prepared to teach, for he holds both Bachelor and Master of Education degrees. However, the most memorable aspect of his classroom presence is his heart. He cares deeply about each one of his students and is there for them both now and in the future. Through the persona of Little A, Chipley gives the boys a fictional character with whom they can identify. Little A's life style echoes theirs. While reading this series of books, the boys witness someone they can relate to. Little A is a wonderful fictional character full of wisdom, character, adventure, and confidence.

Printed in the United States
by Baker & Taylor Publisher Services